Global Insights 1994

John D. Daniels
Indiana University

Lee H. Radebaugh
Brigham Young University

ADDISON-WESLEY PUBLISHING COMPANY

Reading, Massachusetts ▪ Menlo Park, California ▪ New York ▪ Don Mills, Ontario
Wokingham, England ▪ Amsterdam ▪ Bonn ▪ Sydney ▪ Singapore
Tokyo ▪ Madrid ▪ San Juan ▪ Milan ▪ Paris

Sponsoring Editor: Beth Toland
Assistant Editor: Janice Jutras
Permissions Editor: Mary Dyer
Production Supervisor: Kathy Diamond
Freelance Production Coordinator: Ann Kilbride
Text Composition: Winnemay Group
Prepress Consultant: John Webber
Cover Coordinator: Peter Blaiwas
Senior Manufacturing Coordinator: Judy Sullivan

Library of Congress Cataloging-in-Publication Data

Daniels, John D.
    Global Insights, 1994 / by John D. Daniels, Lee H. Radebaugh.
        p. cm.
    ISBN 0-201-59658-X
    1. International economic relations. 2. International trade.
3. International Business enterprises. 4. Environmental policy.
I. Radebaugh, Lee H. II. Title
HF1359.D357 1994   93-25875.
337—dc20   CIP

ISBN 0-201-59658-X

Copyright © 1994 by Addison-Wesley Publishing Company, Inc.

1 2 3 4 5 6 7 8 9 10-AL-9 7 9 6 9 5 9 4 9 3

PREFACE

Since we published the sixth edition of *International Business* in October 1992, there has been a dramatic increase in the number of critical global developments. We've seen changes in national borders, a rising number of ethnic conflicts, an increased focus on the environment, and the emerging importance of strategic alliances in high technology. *Global Insights 1994* has emerged from the need to bridge readers of the updated sixth edition to the current world situation.

Global Insights 1994 is a collection of 16 articles selected from relevant sources such as *Business Week, The Wall Street Journal, The New York Times,* and *Finance & Development*. These articles contain detailed coverage of today's most compelling international business topics. We've provided a broad range of information covering issues in such areas as:

- International Business Ethics
- Environmental Developments
- NAFTA
- Economic Integration in Europe
- Changing Conditions in the Former Soviet Union
- GATT Negotiations
- Developments in Asia, Latin America, and Africa
- Corporate Decisions in a Global Environment
- Changing Role of Multinationals

Our goal is to heighten both the awareness and interest of students to our changing world and the historical events that are unfolding all around us. The articles bring a sense of urgency and immediacy to the classroom, and they expand on the coverage provided in the text.

An introduction to each article directly links each topic to corresponding chapters and page number(s) in the updated sixth edition. You may want to use these articles to:

- Update the conceptual foundations provided by the updated sixth edition
- Stimulate class discussions
- Prepare written assignments by individuals and groups on current events

We hope that you find *Global Insights 1994* a valuable addition to your study of international business. We would like to continue to offer you both creative and challenging ways to enhance the learning of international business. As always, we welcome your feedback and insight to serve better the practical needs of both students and professors.

Indiana University   J.D.D
Brigham Young University   L.H.R

CONTENTS

Global Insights 1994

ARTICLE 1

INTERNATIONAL ETHICAL DILEMMAS

In international business, one needs to be aware of cultural differences that lead to clashes among values. When these clashes occur, decision-makers face the dilemmas of whether to enforce their own values abroad or to adapt to foreign conditions. The following article outlines how value systems may differ and offers a three-stage approach for dealing with differences.

Relationship to text

◆◆ Chapter 3, most of the chapter, but especially page 103, "Ethics and Etiquette," and pages 109–112, "Change Agent or Changed Agent?"

◆◆ Chapter 12, pages 446–448, "Extraterritoriality," and pages 451–453, "Bribery"

◆◆ Chapter 13, pages 483–484, "Codes of Conduct"

After studying the text, reading the article, and answering the questions, you should be able to:

◆◆ Recognize that value differences among countries are inherent and that not all ethical dilemmas can be overcome.

◆◆ Understand some of the major areas of conflict among values when conducting international business.

◆◆ Discern ways to handle conflicts in values.

Preview

◆ Normal business practices representing a group's ethical values may conflict with the home-country values of an international firm abroad.

◆ One dilemma occurs when the end result of an international business transaction can be self-justified ethically, but the means to reach the end cannot be justified.

◆ By understanding the underlying reasons for differences in values, one may find alternative means to satisfy the underlying rationales without violating values of either party.

◆ After identifying the situation and dilemmas, a decision-maker should evaluate options before taking actions.

Adapting Ethical Decisions to a Global Marketplace

A smaller planet has put nations and peoples face-to-face as never before. Only now are we coming to grips with how intertwined our customs and values really are. They are as different yet proximate as camels loping by Abram tanks in the desert; mud-and-thatch huts only minutes away from million-dollar suburban homes; or foreign nationals graduating from Harvard Business School and returning to villages in Yemen or Panama, while their American counterparts interview for Xerox and Citicorp in Manhattan.

In part of Africa, a "family" celebration at the conclusion of a business deal—a party for which you are asked to pay—may well be a sign of friendship and lasting business relationships, not a personal payoff. "Grease" payments to customs officials in some countries may be part of their earning a living wage—not blackmail. In a large number of countries, custom, law and religion support the fact that women are denied personal and professional rights of equality.

Each of these practices is part of some group's ethical standards and affects business dealings between you and the group's members.

Each of these practices also represents a problem of differences—a conflict of values and norms among stakeholders—but not necessarily of right versus

wrong, truth against falsehood or knowledge encountering ignorance. It is certainly not a question of our "good ethics" versus their "bad ethics." Such a view begs the integrity question, but more important, it risks destroying any sense of cooperation based on mutual trust and goodwill.

The real challenge is to bridge differences and value gaps, and hurdle our own perceived obstacles (see related story in MR April 1992, page 42). In today's world, there is much to be accomplished and mutually gained through understanding and respect across cultural lines. The opportunities are there, but so is the clash of values and interests.

A basic step in finding practical solutions to cultural challenges in a global market is to answer two initial questions: First, do you accept the premise that most decisions involve both business and ethics? Second, are you an American businessperson or member of an organization that happens to do business overseas, or are you a global businessperson or member of an organization that happens to have headquarters in the United States?

Your answer to the first question embodies a key philosophical commitment. An affirmative answer means adoption of primary working values and principles—like the health and welfare of customers—from

which action decisions will be made. Your answer to the second question determines a key responsibility commitment; it makes other countries and peoples either valued stakeholder partners or just potential profit centers and resource sites.

Stakeholder Viewpoints

Another step toward better global decision making is to be aware of, and acknowledge, the clash among different cultures, values and principles. This acknowledgment is really a process of learning about other cultures without making business or moral judgments based solely on American customs and mores. You should know the historical, ethnic, cultural, political, legal and religious facts about a country or region, as these facts influence the way the people think, interact and do business. Then you should allow those facts to affect your thinking and acting.

Acknowledgment of the differences between peoples should also include a tolerance of diversity. Our values, beliefs, customs and ethics are not the only acceptable ones. Many nations have value systems that did not evolve from Graeco-Roman and Anglo-Saxon roots, which emphasize the rule of law. Americans easily forget how relatively young and unique the U.S. Constitution and Bill of

Working With Your Principle—And Theirs

Awareness and acknowledgment of differences in values among regions should bring about changes in your thinking and initiatives.

Practices you view as questionable, illegal or simply exploitative may be revealed as local tradition, courtesy and even friendship. I'm not suggesting that you break or ignore your own country's laws or those of other nations. Nor am I condoning begging, blackmail or bribery. This would spell financial, legal and ethical trouble for you, your organization and possibly those of other countries. But you can take initiatives other than outright rejection of legitimate values different from yours on the one hand, or completely selling out your own values on the other.

You can capitalize on new and existing opportunities for business in the following general ways:

1. Become more sensitive to the customs, values and practices of other peoples, which they themselves view as moral, traditional, practical and effective.
2. Don't judge the business customs of others—when different from your own—as necessarily immoral, corrupt, primitive or unworkable. Assume they are legitimate and workable until proved otherwise.

3. Find legitimate ways to operate from their ethical and commercial points of view; do not demand that they operate only by your ground rules.
4. Avoid rationalizing borderline actions, which usually are justified by the following:

   - "This isn't really illegal or immoral."
   - "This is in the organization's and my best interest."
   - "We're safe; no one will find us out."
   - "The organization will condone this and protect me."

5. Refuse to do business when stakeholder options violate or seriously compromise laws or fundamental organizational values.
6. Conduct relationships and negotiations as openly and aboveboard as possible—including reports to stakeholders and public accountability.
7. Avoid purely legalistic but ethically questionable strategies, such as calling "agents" (who are accountable to employers) "distributors" (who are not).

Rights are. Indeed, most other systems were practiced for centuries before the United States existed.

The values and customs of other nations are not necessarily primitive, degraded or wrong because they are different from ours. Hence, they don't call for our immediate suspicion, distrust or condemnation. Until proved otherwise, they are only different—having evolved under distinct geographies, conditions and heritages.

By example, let's look at the practical problems of bribery and payoffs. Most foreign governments, including many well known for corruption, have enforced statutes against most forms of private payoff. Yet in some countries of Africa, ancient traditions take precedence over law. Payoffs have become the norm and are rooted in a "communal heritage," in which a community leader's wealth was shared with the community; those who hoarded were scorned. The Nigerian practice of "dash"—private pay for private service—traces back to trade in the form of gifts exchanged for labor.

American organizations frequently deal through foreign nationals who have been educated in the United States, know American

business ways, but are very much a part of their own culture. They may hold seemingly conflicting values: some instilled in the West, others a part of their local tradition and life. They may see no conflict in negotiating along Western lines and then reverting to communal traditions when discussing more private remuneration. These people need not be labeled completely corrupt; rather, they are drawn by both indigenous and Western values. They may have American ideals of personal business enrichment and want to adhere to communal obligations at the same time.

If you are involved in business with Third World countries,

you need to understand three widespread traditions that affect business transactions and added remunerations: the inner circle, future favors and the gift exchange.

Inner Circle Communal societies divide people into two groups: Those with whom they have relationships, and those with whom they have none—the goal being group prosperity and protection. There are the "in" people and the "out" people. The "ins" are family; the "outs" are strangers. In East and West Africa, inner circles can be true relatives, comrades or persons of similar age or region. In China, they may be those who share the same dialect; in India, members of the same caste. These are not unlike the "old boy networks" in the United States. The effect in many of these countries is to restrict social and business dealings to those with whom the businessperson has safe, trusting relationships. Often that trust is forthcoming if Westerners willing to honor communal values become part of the inner circle.

Future Favors The system of future favors operates within the inner circles. In Japan it is known as "inner duty," in Kenya, "inner relationship," and in the Philippines, "inner debt." In these traditions, the person obligated to another is expected to repay the favor sometime in the future. Some form of favor or service will repay the earlier debt; this repayment then places the grantor of the original favor under future obligation. Lifelong shifting obligations create relationships of trust and are the basis for doing business.

Gift Exchange In many non-Western circles, the gift exchange tradition has evolved into a business tool: Gifts begin a process of future favors. They are

an immediate sign of gratitude or hospitality, but upon acceptance, they generate an obligation that the recipient must someday repay.

Inner Circles, future favors and gift exchanges exist in American society also, but they don't usually have the same sense of obligation—either in the present or in the future. Nor is there the same sense of "family" with ensuing trust or loyalty present. Rather, many Americans feel a sense of ethical wariness when the relationship seems to move beyond gratitude, courtesy or friendliness to even remotely suggest influence in decision making.

The Results System

Looking closely at the consequences of foreign practices rather than the actions themselves can clarify difficult situations. Gift giving is a good example. Solicitation of gifts has no place in U.S. business circles when it smacks of exploitation. This may be true in other countries too, but foreign colleagues often are at a loss to know how to initiate honorable, lasting relationships that form around business ventures—especially when Americans have little time for social amenities, are ignorant of local traditions or are wary of the exchange of gifts that creates obligations and trust.

Foreigners often take on the role of initial giver or may suggest that gift giving is the traditional way of entering the local business system. This role is viewed as a courteous and acceptable means of furthering business. You should look at the true purpose and legitimate consequences of such gift giving, considered in a local context other than your own.

An American company that exclusively manufactured and distributed medical devices for human implantation was asked for payment outside the contract; if it did not comply, it would lose the right to sell in a certain foreign country. The company had to weigh payment to certain non-governmental parties against its business interests as well as the life-and-death need of hundreds of citizens who could not obtain the device by any other means. Weighing the good consequences of an action against a questionably ethical "means to the end" makes for a tough call. Yet a decision for remuneration in some form could well be the right one, given the importance of the devices versus an unwanted but unavoidable payment.

The Responsibility System

A promise to respond to important stakeholders in a spirit of cooperation also allows for new initiatives in doing business in foreign countries. Whereas directly granting requests for private monies exposes U.S. organizations to financial and legal threats, invoking the principle of responsibility to—but not for—other stakeholders makes alternate answers appropriate. Nonmonetary public service benefits could well replace payoffs and satisfy the needs of both sides, for instance.

I wonder if the specter of foreign payoffs and bribes doesn't sometimes blind American organizations to the fact that technical expertise, follow-up satisfaction and customer service also are powerful incentives to buy. Responsibility to the customer through quality, partnering and service is the name of the game today. It has top

The Magnificent Seven Principles

1. **Dignity Of Human Life.** The lives of people are to be respected. Human beings, by the fact of their existence, have value and dignity. We may not act in ways that directly intend to harm an innocent person. Human beings have a right to live; we have an obligation to respect that right to life. Human life is to be preserved and treated as sacred.

2. **Autonomy.** All persons are intrinsically valuable and have the right to self-determination. We should act in ways that demonstrate each person's worth, dignity, and right to free choice. We have a right to act in ways that assert our own worth and legitimate needs. We should not use others as mere "things," or only as means to an end. Each person has an equal right to basic human liberty, compatible with a similar liberty for others.

3. **Honesty.** The truth should be told to those who have a right to know it. Honesty is also known as integrity, truth-telling and honor. One should speak and act so as to reflect the reality of the situation. Speaking and acting should mirror the way things really are. There are times when others have the right to hear the truth from us; there are times when they do not.

4. **Loyalty.** Promises, contracts and commitments should be honored. Loyalty includes fidelity, promise keeping, maintaining the public trust, good citizenship, excellence in quality of work, reliability, commitment, and honoring just laws, rules and policies. One

should honor and keep confidences, proprietary information and personal private information that is freely and willingly shared. People should fulfill written and verbal contracts and commitments. They should fulfill just rules, laws and policies.

5. **Fairness.** People should be treated justly. People have the right to be treated fairly, impartially and equitably. People also have the obligation to treat others fairly and justly. Everyone has the right to the necessities of life. Justice includes equal, unbiased treatment. Fairness tolerates diversity and accepts differences in people and their ideas. All employees have the right to fair treatment under work contracts, company policies and procedures, and the law.

6. **Humaneness.** This has two parts: Our actions ought to accomplish good; and we should avoid doing evil. We should do good to others and to ourselves. We should have concern for the well-being of others; usually, we show this concern in the form of compassion, kindness, serving and caring. We should act and speak in ways that benefit our valid self-interests and those of others. We must avoid actions that are evil.

7. **The Common Good.** Actions should accomplish the greatest good for the greatest number of people. One should act and speak in ways that benefit the welfare of the largest number of people, while trying to protect the rights of individuals.

priority within the United States—why not overseas as well? While firmly rejecting direct private payoffs, you may counter with monies clearly directed at needed help to others not touched by the contracts themselves. Even if these funds make the foreign contacts richer, in the long run some portion of the wealth is often shared communally with many relatives and "mates."

In fact, Kenya and Indonesia have made such requests of U.S. companies. It is not uncommon for non-Western colleagues of American organizations to view requests for private monies as a way of helping themselves, but also as a means to aid larger groups and their nations.

Responsibility also may suggest that donations could be open contributions to build schools, hos-

pitals, medical clinics or agricultural projects. Such donations could be directed to the provinces or villages of the foreign counterparts or colleagues. Donating services, tools or machine parts is another alternative to private payoffs. Tanzanian poaching patrols have been helped in this way by British companies, and Coca-Cola hired Egyptians to plant acres of orange trees. Both cases resulted in needed political favor, increased local employment and goodwill.

The object, of course, is self-interest on both sides. But cooperation and goodwill are the responsible means. Public service, donations, employment, social progress and the use of local customs and traditions are far superior to bribes, misunderstanding, or simply walking away from mutual business opportunity and benefit.

America's Foreign Corrupt Practices Act of 1977 (FCPA) prohibits payments to foreign officials, political parties or candidates for the purpose of influencing an act or decision intended to obtain or retain business. Companies and their managers also are liable if they know, or had reason to know, that their agents used payments from a U.S. concern to pay foreign officials for a prohibited purpose.

Nowhere does the FCPA prohibit the use of funds to aid developing societies. You and your organization often can solve ethical/business dilemmas by turning potential private payoffs into public services. Such decisions then would be openly defensible and justifiable on ethical as well as legal grounds—a powerful argument.

Three-Step Process

Ultimately, you will want to apply the following process to issues or dilemmas posed in the global marketplace:

1. Examine the situation. Acknowledgment of the histories, customs and values of the people involved gives added insight into the critical facts of the situation. You will be better able to identify the key stakeholders, who may be more numerous than in the United States. Communal traditions, inner circle relationships, and other non-Western colleagues lengthen the list.

2. Establish the dilemma. Identify the working principles and norms that drive each of the stakeholder options (i.e., why they want their options chosen). Since foreign values and principles are likely to differ from those you quickly assign to American clients, this will help you focus the issue or dilemma.

With a more balanced acknowledgment of why foreigners hold certain values and "stakes" when approaching business, you will better understand their intentions. Projecting the outcomes of the stakeholders' options should then be closer to reality and less colored by your own values and principles.

Then you can attempt to determine the actions that stakeholders will take to produce the outcome they want. At this point, ask whether those actions, as means to the end, violate your own or organizational principles. You may see significant clashes of your principles, your organization's principles, and your laws with theirs. But you also will find common values.

Awareness of their values and customs will help you judge more accurately and fairly whether the means they will use in fulfillment of their options are acceptable or unacceptable ground rules for you.

3. Evaluate the options. The key to value-based decision making is to choose an option for action that flows from business values and principles rooted responsibly in the Magnificent Seven General Principles (see box). Given your awareness of the similarities and differences in interpretation of these principles by other people, identify which principle is driving each stakeholder option, including your own.

Finally, compare the General Principles behind each option. Which is the most responsible principle in this situation? The answer to this question will come as a result of weighing the General Principles that drive all the options.

Moving Forward

Awareness and acknowledgment of differences, respect for traditions other than your own, changes in thinking and in initiatives, principled and responsible decisions flowing from a practical decision-making process—all these will help open the door to waiting opportunities.

It would be naive to think that all the differences and contradictions between our business and ethical systems can be overcome to the mutual satisfaction of all. Some differences will never be reconciled.

No country or its businesspeople should have to sell out to another. But Americans have not been sensitive and open enough to business and ethical systems other than our own. While different from yours and mine in many ways, the cultures and customs of other countries are not beyond a working spirit of what we both would call, in our own ways, cooperation and shared moral responsibility.

QUESTIONS

1. List a group of practices that may differ between your own country and some foreign country. For which would you have the most difficulty adjusting to norms in the foreign country? Why?

2. Are there any values that you would consider universal? What are they?

3. Do you see any ethical dilemmas in the implementation of the "magnificent seven principles" explained in the article?

4. How might you ascertain value differences for a foreign country?

ARTICLE 2

KEY ENVIRONMENTAL ISSUES

The 1990s are being called the decade of the environment, and environmental issues may play a major role in trade and other international relationships long beyond the year 2000. The short article, "Rio Baedeker: A Layman's Guide to Key Environmental Issues," reviews the major viewpoints that were discussed at the 1992 global conference in Rio de Janeiro, Brazil.

Relationship to text

◆◆ Chapter 5, pages 171–174, "Industrialization Objectives," and pages 176–177, "Fairness"

◆◆ Chapter 9, pages 329–330, "The World Bank"

◆◆ Chapter 10, pages 354–355, "Models of Successful Market Economies"

◆◆ Chapter 11, pages 419–420, "The Environment"

After studying the text, reading the article, and answering the questions, you should be able to:

◆◆ Describe the major environmental issues that affect global economic relationships.

◆◆ Contrast the optimistic and pessimistic views on the future of the global environment.

◆◆ Understand the place of environmental protection within national objectives.

◆◆ Relate how differences among nations in environmental protection may lead to conflicts affecting international business.

Preview

◆ The four major issues addressed at the Rio conference were over-population, biodiversity, deforestation, and ocean pollution.

◆ People take widely contrasting views on whether certain environmental conditions are problems and, if problems, what to do about them.

Rio Baedeker

A Layman's Guide to Key Environmental Issues

	Description	Pessimist's View	Optimist's View	Likely Outcome
Over-Population	Now at 5.4 billion, the world's population is growing by about 95 million a year. If current trends continue, world population could nearly triple to 14 billion by the latter half of the next century.	Overpopulation worsens poverty, accelerates pollution, jeopardizes food supplies, spreads disease, Failure to curb population growth undermines economic progress and magnifies environmental decline.	Population growth is a natural partner of economic progress. The world's carrying capacity is vast, and natural resources are abundant. Technology and human ingenuity can solve any serious shortages, if they arise.	At the summit, many groups will advocate more contraceptive research and greater spending on voluntary family planning programs. But resistance from religious conservatives will probably preclude substantive action.
Biodiversity	Human activities continue to reduce biological diversity. Extinction rates are accelerating. Among the causes: poverty, pollution, excessive exploitation, habitat destruction and the introduction of alien species.	As economic development spreads, ecosystem are chopped into ever-smaller fragments, able to support fewer species. Genetic material–for example, specimens of individual species–need to be protected and managed as sovereign resources.	Extinction of species from time to time is part of nature's way. Biotechnology and business need unfettered access to the world's natural resources to support scientific progress and economic growth.	Negotiators from 98 countries favor new policies to promote biodiversity, but the U.S. and some other wealthy nations oppose promises of aid to poor countries without making them take conservation actions on their own.
Deforestation	Forests are reeling from pressures of economic development. Clear-cutting destroys habitat and watersheds, increases erosion and reduces the world's ability to cope with greenhouse gases.	Deforestation threatens the entire planet. More than 90% of the world's land-dwelling plants and animals inhabit forest. Tropical deforestation is accelerating.	Trees are renewable resource and the supply is abundant. Selective cutting of the forests brings needed jobs and income, spurring further economic development.	Binding agreements on forest protection appear remote. Developing countries oppose restrictions on their forestry practices unless they are compensated for their stewardship.
Ocean	The single greatest threat to the world's oceans is pollution from land-based sources, which account for about 70% of all the toxic chemicals, sediment, garbage and other pollutants at sea.	As toxic algae blooms spread, they deplete oxygen and block sunlight, killing fish and other life forms. Alarming threats are also posed by alien species introduced as cargo ships routinely discharge ballast water in foreign harbors.	The capacity of the ocean to "cleanse" themselves is enormous. Besides, most ocean pollution from land-based sources can be managed effectively by individual nations and through bilateral and regional arrangements.	Proponents of ocean protection will press for legal curbs on land-based pollution. So far, 45 nations have ratified the Law of the Sea agreement, created in 1982, but commitments from 15 more are needed to put it in force . The U.S. will probably remain an influential holdout.

WALL STREET JOURNAL: "Rio Baedeker: A Layman's Guide to Key Environmental Issues," June 3, 1992, p. B1. Reprinted by permission of *The Wall Street Journal*, © 1992 Dow Jones & Co., Inc. All Rights Reserved Worldwide.

QUESTIONS

1. What difference does it make if another nation takes less stringent action to protect the environment than one's own country takes?

2. Part of the Law of the Sea agreement calls for global ownership of minerals that are outside the confines of any nation's territory. Why do you think the United States and some other industrial countries have objected to this provision and have refused to sign the agreement?

3. Why would developing countries object to the protection of their forests?

4. Will more stringent population controls help poor countries to develop economically?

ARTICLE 3

ECONOMIC GROWTH WITH ENVIRONMENTAL PROTECTION

The Rio Conference brought together business, government, and environmental groups for the first time. The Summit was not entirely successful, since many key issues relating to sustainable development were not addressed. It did result in a psychological boost to the cooperative nature of environmental discussions. This article discusses issues that governments need to address to help create sustainable development—development that links economic growth and environmental protection.

Relationship to text

◆◆ Chapter 2, pages 62–64, "Key Economic Issues in Industrial and Developing Countries"

After studying the text, reading the article, and answering the questions, you should be able to:

◆◆ Define the concept, "sustainable development."

◆◆ Identify some of the problems with the Rio Summit.

◆◆ Discuss some of the major benefits from the Summit from the standpoint of business/government discussions.

◆◆ Identify some of the policies that government can implement to assist sustainable development.

Preview

◆ The Rio Summit was disappointing to most observers and participants, containing little that was concrete or innovative.

◆ A large amount of money is needed to manage effectively environmental resources in developing countries.

◆ Businesses must learn to produce more goods and services using fewer resources and creating less pollution.

◆ Rio produced an agenda for change and focused the attention of leaders worldwide on critical issues.

◆ Rio brought business into the development and environment decision-making arena.

The Business of Sustainable Development

Protecting the environment and pursuing profits are normally perceived as being at odds with each other. But Stephan Schmidheiny, a Swiss industrialist, has long disputed this view. In the summer of 1990, he was asked by Maurice Strong, the secretary general of the then planned "Earth Summit" in Rio de Janeiro, to develop a business perspective for the Summit and to interest fellow business leaders around the world in the concept of "sustainable development." Mr. Schmidheiny responded by forming the Business Council for Sustainable Development (BCSD), which brought together 48 chief executives of major corporations worldwide.

Shortly before the Summit opened in June 1992, the BCSD published a sort of business "manifesto"—a 350-page book called Changing Course. It called for a new partnership among government, business, and society, based on the recognition that "economic growth and environmental protection are inextricably linked, and that the quality of present and future life rests on meeting basic human needs without destroying the environment on which all life depends." Controversial proposals included greater reliance on economic instruments such as pollution taxes, and gradually abolishing subsidies for coal and electricity.

With the June 1992 Earth Summit now behind us, *Finance & Development* asked Mr. Schmidheiny, who served as the principal adviser for business and industry to Mr. Strong, what he thought of the outcome of Rio. What steps are next if private industry is to join hands with governments in ensuring that present needs are met in ways that do not compromise future generations and that make sound business sense?

It is impossible to predict how historians will judge the Earth Summit in Rio. But among its many products, the United Nations Conference on Environment and Development (UNCED), to give it its official title, generated seven tons of waste per day, most of this consisting of discarded reports, drafts, bulletins, and memos. Given that the Summit's final documents were disappointing to most observers and participants, containing little that was concrete or innovative, this is an impressive amount of pollution.

Unfortunately, many of the issues that must be discussed in any informed debate on sustainable development population, trade, security, and debt—were either not on the agenda or received only vague lip service. On the other hand, diplomats of virtually all governments spent months preparing for the conference, which necessitated learning the rudiments of sustainability. Over one hundred national leaders had to decide what the ideal meant to them and their people.

In the end, we may decide that the Summit's real value was in its long-term psychological impact, not the scant immediate legal or financial contributions. Indeed, we may look back to Rio as, not the beginning, but "the end of the beginning" of a change of course toward economic and political systems compatible with environmental realities. That process of beginning lasted two decades—from Stockholm (with the 1972 UN Conference on the Human Environment, the first time world leaders came together to consider the fate of the planet) to Rio.

As for my own view of the Summit, it is, quite naturally, tempered by a business perspective, and from that perspective, I believe Rio was a key turning point in human affairs. The United Nations and member governments finally summoned up the realism to include business in their deliberations, and business finally summoned up the vision to see that its open participation in such deliberations is in its own and the world's best interests.

To see what a breakthrough this is, one need only look at past conferences. Stockholm '72 attempted to solve environmental problems with virtually no representation from business—the primary polluter and primary user of resources. And countless conferences on "development" have sought ways to help poor countries progress without any real participation by business, the key creator of wealth, jobs, income, and opportunity. Of course, it must be admitted that business, in its meetings and conferences, has not traditionally shown any desire to get involved in environment and development issues, except defensively.

A Conducive Environment

Much of the debate at Rio centered on increased flows of development assistance. In a sense, this was understandable, as there is no doubt that sustainable development will require massive financing throughout the world, or that levels of development assistance must increase. But neither is there any doubt that aid flows will never be enough to get the job done.

Thus, the large amounts of money needed to effectively manage environmental resources in the developing world, lift peo-

ple out of poverty, and provide for rapidly growing populations will have to come from economic growth, domestic savings, and wise investments at the national and international level. Foreign investment capital must be attracted, but today only a few developing countries are managing to do this. Of the 18 percent of foreign investments that flowed to developing countries in the second half of the 1980s, about 75 percent went to only ten countries mostly in Asia and Latin America. Net capital inflows into Latin America rose from $9.6 billion in 1989 to $18.4 billion in 1990, and then doubled again in 1991 to $36 billion—a sharp upward trend that continued in 1992.

Latin America has benefited from new policy frameworks—in particular, legal and institutional changes—that served to strengthen the private sector. Typical actions included the elimination of most ownership restrictions on properties, other forms of deregulation and privatization, and the removal of trade barriers. Many countries in Latin America and elsewhere are finally beginning to clarify property rights, making them available to small farmers in a straightforward and streamlined manner. Clear property rights were a key ingredient in Zimbabwe's maize miracle in the early 1980s, and they have helped improve the productivity of small farms in Indonesia and Thailand.

Increasingly, we see that given the right signals and support, industrial and developing country businesses with common interests will seek out long-term partnerships with one another, a process that helps transfer skills and competitiveness across borders. But governments— in both industrial and developing nations—must clearly understand

that private industry can be a force for sustainable development only when it is allowed to act as private industry should. That means not being saddled with public sector chores, such as creating jobs, and not being expected to operate on concessional terms, but being encouraged to internalize environmental costs.

The New Partnership

When I spoke to the plenary in Rio, I found myself delivering a message that is inherent in Changing Course, but not as boldly stated as it should have been. I called for a bold new partnership between business and governments, noting that "business must move beyond the traditional approach of backdoor lobbying; governments must move beyond traditional overreliance on command-and-control regulations."

In recent years, it has become increasingly obvious what sorts of actions are required of governments to move toward more sustainable forms of progress. Moreover, the sorts of steps required of business are ever more self-evident—that is, producing ever more goods and services using fewer resources and creating less pollution. But not enough attention has been focused on trying to work out how government and business can cooperate on the key tasks at hand.

Most of my recommendations here are for governments. This does not imply, however, that business does not need to change radically. Many companies are already becoming more "ecologically efficient" as they respond to a number of pressures: "green" consumerism; media emphasis on the environment; banks' greater willingness to lend to—

and insurance companies' greater willingness to cover—companies that will not face big clean-up bills or lawsuits; internal pressure from employees; tougher regulations; new environmental taxes and changes; and plain old senses of corporate and personal responsibility. But business as a whole will not change for the better until the market framework in which business operates sends different signals—that make economic and environmental excellence inseparable.

Reforming Macroeconomic And Political Systems

One of the first tasks for developing country governments is to create free competitive markets, thereby improving efficiency and the allocation of scarce resources. The goal must be to attract investment from outside and create opportunities inside—particularly opportunities for members of the "informal" sector to both join in and thrive in the formal sector.

But macroeconomic reforms must be accompanied by political changes toward participatory democracy. Effective participation in political decision making and effective participation in market decision making appear to go hand-in-hand, eventually. The new democracies of Eastern Europe are seeking to establish open markets. And the citizens of the newly industrialized economies of Asia, having participated in business prosperity, are clamoring for increased democracy. Certainly effective environmental decision making requires a people free to organize themselves into pressure groups, a free media, and freedom to vote for new leaders. Also, as the real "environmental decision makers" are the people making daily decisions in forests, fields, and factories, then they must feel that they have a say in setting environmental rules.

The rules of doing business will be most efficiently changed if business leaders play a leading role in the process. At Rio, the BCSD released a lengthy report, largely put together by African business leaders, on the need for change in that continent, including many case studies showing how business is helping. BCSD members in Latin America produced their own book on how "the rules of the game" must be changed and how they will participate in that process. We have also encouraged the establishment of national BCSDs in several developing countries and hope many more are set up in the months and years ahead.

Pricing Changes

Another urgent task—and this one applies to developed and developing countries alike—is to reform the fiscal systems in such a way that natural resources and pollution have more appropriate (usually higher) prices. Here the evidence increasingly shows that the answer lies in finding an optimal mix of regulations, self-regulation, and economic instruments.

The more forward-thinking governments are trying to develop economic instruments that better blend market realities and environmental realities (for example, pollution taxes and tradable permits). Such instruments are usually more efficient than command-and-control regulations (emission standards and mandated technical standards), although there will always be a role for these, particularly where health is threatened or damage may be severe and permanent. A few of the more forward-thinking companies are attempting to regulate themselves now, so as to avoid the necessity of being regulated by governments later.

But establishing this optimal mix will require public-private cooperation everywhere, particu-

larly in the developing world. How could this work? One example might be in the area of regulation: Most developing countries either have too few or too unrealistic regulations, besides lacking sufficient trained regulators and enforcement capacity. Suppose multinational corporations, skilled in dealing with regulations in industrial countries, made available pro bono their expertise in working with regulators in developing countries. These companies might also help these governments establish regulations and economic instruments that are realistic and enforceable.

This would be advantageous for both the companies and the governments. Indeed, Eastern Europe has shown the tragedy that can result from a combination of rigorous but rarely enforced regulations. Governments, companies, and perhaps a multilateral organization like the UN Development Programme, or the World Bank's Global Environment Facility, might even develop a set of "model" baseline regulations that would be suitable for countries at different stages of development.

Redesigning National Accounts

Another largely government job in which business should play a role is the development of integrated environmental and economic accounts to reflect both damages to and improvements in stocks of natural resources and in ecosystems. This would provide a better statistical data base for economic analysis and indirectly encourage better policymaking.

The task will not be easy, however, as demonstrated in two recent studies carried out by the UN Statistical Division and the World Bank, which highlighted problems of data availability, as well as conceptual and empirical valuation issues. In the case of Papua New Guinea, the researchers found that when depreciation of capital, including natural resources, was included in GDP calculations, economic growth from 1986–90 was reduced by between 1–11 percent, depending on the year chosen and the method used. For Mexico, the GDP reduction ranged from 11–23 percent. Nonetheless, the UN Statistical Commission is expected to give the green light to environmentally adjusted accounting at its February 1993 meeting.

Business could feed into this process by measuring environmental performance, conducting its own regular environmental audits and assessments of compliance, and periodically providing appropriate information to boards of directors, shareholders, employees, national authorities, and the general public. Given that such accounting may change their bottom line (that is, reduce profits and/or result in smaller asset balances), public pressure and the development of environmentally oriented accounting standards may be needed. The same accounting rules must apply to all companies

Technology Cooperation

The requirement for clean, equitable economic growth, especially in the developing world, remains the single greatest problem within the larger challenge of sustainable development. A cost-effective way to achieve this would be through business-to-business "technology cooperation," which focuses on the development of business, in the process building up the infrastructure, wealth-generating capacity, and competitiveness of a country. It works best through long-term partnerships that ensure that both parties benefit by commitment to the continued success of the project.

One critical way that technology cooperation helps developing countries is through the transfer of "software," which is just as important as the "hardware." Software here refers not only to the know-how, operating, and maintenance skills associated with the technology but also adaptations appropriate to the cultural context and experience of the receiving organization and the society that is going to use it.

But business-to-business technology cooperation calls for—indeed, in the poorest countries, demands—a new partnership between business and government. Private sector investment and development assistance, both bilateral and multilateral, should support long-term commercial financing and create projects that are part commercial and part concessional. Government financing and business training schemes should support the necessary capacity building. It is easy to imagine five-way partnerships: a business in the North and a business in the South, a government in the North and a government in the South, and a multilateral, perhaps a UN, body helping to broker the cooperation.

Managing Renewable Resources
Finally, we come to farming and forestry, two areas where the BCSD is paying a great deal of attention, as they sustain the livelihoods of almost half this planet's people and have extensive, direct impacts on the environment. Too many farming activities in the industrial world and parts of the developing world are affected by subsidies that encourage damaging patterns of resource use. As a first step, distorting subsidies that encourage the overuse of such inputs as water, fertilizers, and pesticides, should be gradually removed.

In the developing world, farmers rarely have the political power or economic power appropriate to

their numbers or their contribution to national economies. Empowerment certainly does not guarantee more efficient natural resource management; but powerless farmers have neither the means nor the motivation to get involved in the hard work of soil or water conservation, for example. On the development side, where farmers have gained access to markets, credit, improved seeds, and other inputs, crop yields have often increased dramatically.

As for forestry, about three quarters of the planet's forests have been brought under government ownership in the past two decades. Certainly, governments have an appropriate role to play in protecting and conserving important forest ecosystems in the form of national parks and other protected areas. However, governments have rarely proved themselves effective in running forestry enterprises for timber production. This is best left to the private sector. But if business is to replant forests, create plantations, and respect the ecological services of forests and the needs of all human inhabitants, they will need new systems of regulations and economic instruments. For example, the tax systems of many Scandinavian countries encourage the replanting of forests, even though the trees may take 100 years to mature, while the tax systems of many developing nations encourage forest destruction.

How To Proceed

I am not in any of the above instances arguing for a "leave it to business" approach. Clearly business, by itself, cannot provide all the answers. But I do believe we have yet to define what business does best and what governments do best. And I do believe that given the present environmental and developmental crisis, we must sort this out urgently and then get on with cooperating on the business of sustainable development.

From my perspective, Rio was a success. It produced an agenda for change, and it focused the attention of leaders worldwide on some critical issues. It also produced the crucial break-through of bringing business into the development and environment decision-making arena. Business has always fueled development and affected the environment—using natural resources, producing pollution, developing and spreading technology, creating terms and paths of trade, and making possible both survival and progress. It is now time that business becomes involved with governments and other non-governmental organizations—in actively and thoughtfully charting the developmental and environmental paths of humankind.

FINANCE & DEVELOPMENT: Stephan Schmidheiny, "The Business of Sustainable Development," *Finance & Development*, December 1992. Reprinted with permission of the International Monetary Fund.

QUESTIONS

1. Why was the Rio Summit disappointing in some ways?

2. In what ways was the Rio Summit a turning point in human affairs?

3. Why should business be closely involved in environmental discussions?

4. Why is a large amount of money needed for the developing countries? Why are they having trouble obtaining those resources?

5. What are some factors causing companies to be more environmentally responsible?

6. What can government do in the following areas to help solve some of the environmental problems?

   ◆ reforming macroeconomic and political systems

   ◆ pricing changes

   ◆ redesigning national accounts

   ◆ technology cooperation

   ◆ managing renewable resources

ARTICLE 4

ETHNIC CONFLICTS AND DOMINANCE

Nation-states have long been recognized as both a cause and effect of ethnic identity. The existence of superpowers and the cold war bolstered nation-states that were not delineated along ethnic lines. With the demise of the cold war, many violent ethnic, religious, and sectional conflicts have surfaced.

Companies face a changing business environment that includes political risk from new wars and insurrections.

Relationship to text

◆◆ Chapter 2, pages 50–51, "Measures of Freedom"

◆◆ Chapter 3, page 88, "The Nation-State as Proxy of Society"

◆◆ Chapter 10, page 360, "National Heterogeneity"

◆◆ Chapter 16, pages 585–588, "Political Risk"

After studying the text, reading the article, and answering the questions, you should be able to:

◆◆ Characterize the relationship between cultural or ethnic groups and nation-states.

◆◆ Explain why the number of nation-states has increased.

◆◆ Outline how the concept of self-determination may affect international business.

◆◆ Summarize suggested proposals dealing with the emergence of ethnic minorities and rivalries.

◆◆ Recount specific examples of countries encountering violence related to ethnic separateness movements.

Preview

◆ Whether people should have self-determination has been debated since World War I.

◆ Ethnic differences have recently led to violence in about a third of the world's nations and have led to wider U.N. peace-keeping operations.

◆ Much global public opinion is in favor of intervention in another nation's affairs to protect the rights of minorities.

As Ethnic Wars Multiply, U.S. Strives for a Policy

In Baring Old Hatreds, the Cold War's End Imperils the Peace

At the height of World War I, Woodrow Wilson argued that self-determination for Europe's myriad ethnic minorities, suddenly freed by the collapse of the Austro-Hungarian and Ottoman Empires, would provide stability in the postwar environment. But even as the concept of self-determination was being born, President Wilson's own Secretary of State, Robert Lansing, worried that the idea might make the world more dangerous.

"Will it not breed discontent, disorder and rebellion?" Lansing wrote. "The phrase is simply loaded with dynamite. It will raise hopes which can never be realized. It will, I fear, cost thousands of lives.

"What a calamity that the phrase was ever uttered! What misery it will cause!"

Now as the cold war gives way to dozens of smaller wars over ethnic dominance, diplomats, scholars and world leaders alike are coping with the legacy Lansing cautioned against in the second decade of the century.

Policy makers say that the current ethnic conflicts are actually the third wave of this century, with the first two having taken place after World War I and the explosion of anticolonial movements in Africa and Asia after World War II. But the newest wave is seen as even more complex, potentially more threatening to international peace and almost certain to grow in the years ahead.

U.S. Seeking Options

Indeed, diplomats and scholars inside and outside the Clinton Administration have begun studying options to deal with the new kinds of conflicts that range from enhancing the role of the United Nations to establishing a new international tribunal to listen to grievances by ethnic minorities in various countries.

Citing what he called "the surfacing of long-suppressed ethnic, religious and sectional conflicts" in the world, Secretary of State Warren Christopher said before taking office that the task of heading off such rivalries would be a primary objective for the United States.

"If we don't find some way that the different ethnic groups can live together in a country, how many countries will we have?" Mr. Christopher said at confirmation hearings before the Senate Foreign Relations Committee. "We'll have 5,000 countries rather than the hundred plus we now have."

Mr. Christopher called for "preventive diplomacy" to keep the conflicts from spreading. He also endorsed "new dispute resolution techniques," including some form of international arbitration, and increased use of United Nations forces to monitor and enforce agreements.

"We can't afford to career from crisis to crisis," Mr. Christopher said. "We must have a new diplomacy that can anticipate and prevent crises, like those in Iraq and Bosnia and Somalia, rather than simply manage them."

The Secretary's testimony might be seen by some as contradicting one Administration policy—namely, its refusal to endorse the plan put forward by a joint mediation effort led by Cyrus R. Vance, the United Nations negotiator, and Lord Owen, the European Community envoy, to end the war in Bosnia and Herzegovina. The Clinton Administration is concerned that the negotiators' peace plan to divide Bosnia into 10 regions might reward the Serbian side for its campaign of "ethnic cleansing" against Muslims and Croats.

Enshrined in U.N. Charter

President Wilson's original proposals for self-determination have influenced American policy for generations and were eventually enshrined after World War II in the United Nations Charter. Many diplomats say that the concept is unlikely to be discarded even though there are rising fears that it may be carried to extremes.

"The defining mode of conflict in the era ahead is ethnic conflict," said Senator Daniel Patrick Moynihan, the New York Democrat. "It promises to be savage. Get ready for 50 new countries in the world in the next 50 years. Most of them will be born in bloodshed."

The biggest factor in unleashing the conflicts has been the end of the cold war, in which the superpowers mostly succeeded in suppressing ethnic rivalries within their spheres of influence.

"The nation-state as a European concept has brought together all kinds of elements of diversity, kept in check by state power and hooked into global structures," said Francis M. Deng, a former Foreign Minister in Sudan and now a senior associate at the Brookings Institution.

"Once you remove the cold war factionalism, there is the euphoria of freedom, everyone asserting the identities that were previously suppressed," he said. "We are now witnessing the desire of people to fall back on that which is authentic to them."

Old Grievances at Issue

In many of the conflicts today, Muslims are under attack by other groups—like Serbs in the former Yugoslavia or Hindu militants in India—who assert a sense of grievance nursed after Muslim conquests many centuries ago. But at the same time Islamic fundamentalists are on the attack in Central Asia, the Middle East and Africa, where last week Pope John Paul II appealed to Muslims not to use force to press their doctrines on non-believers.

The question facing policy makers in light of the tensions is how

the United States decides where its interests lie. Scholars and others say that little work has been done to try to assign priorities of where to intervene and where not to.

"I don't think we have a doctrine for the complicated set of circumstances we face," said Michael Krepon, president of the Henry L. Stimson Center, which conducts policy research on arms control and peacemaking. In some cases, he said, warring parties in such conflicts would welcome the presence of an American or other outside intermediary, but in other cases they would oppose such a force.

A new idea is evolving among diplomats to the effect that the international community may have a right to intervene in the affairs of a country simply because that country is mistreating its minority groups. At the very least some say, nations should withhold diplomatic recognition of such countries.

"The international system is at a crossroads on the concept of what is a nation state," Madeleine K. Albright, the United States representative to the United Nations, said in an interview before appointment. "We need to make sure that when a country declares independence, individual as well as minority rights are guaranteed before granting recognition.

U.N. Activities Mushroom

The United Nations is certain to be the focus of stepped-up efforts to deal with international conflicts. Since 1988, 14 new United Nations peacekeeping operations have been established, more than in the previous 40 years of its history. The number of soldiers wearing the United Nations blue berets has risen four-fold this year and the budget for peacekeeping operations jumped from $700 million in 1991 to $2.8 billion in 1992.

In the early years of its activities, the United Nations' main function was to send observer missions or forces to monitor cease-fires. On the new world stage, the United Nations has begun deploying forces as part of political settlements, in some cases helping to disarm the parties in conflict and organize elections to try to bring stability to the war-torn nations. It has carried out such activities in El Salvador, Namibia, Mozambique, Western Sahara, Angola and, in its biggest operation, Cambodia.

"It is fairly clear in some parts of the world that the nation-state is not an adequate expression of the political framework when minorities are automatically disenfranchised," said a senior State Department official involved in such operations. "To a large degree, we have to get away from the idea of total respect for sovereignty that was once sacrosanct."

This official said that Cambodia, Bosnia and Somalia were "states not capable of governing themselves," and that in each, the United States and other United Nations members had begun to "take government powers out of the hands of indigenous peoples."

In all past situations, though, the United Nations or outside forces went in with the full consent of the parties in conflict. What is facing it now is whether to go into cases where it might forcefully have to disarm one side.

An Old Idea Is Revived

Others suggest that the United Nations should go even further and in effect run countries that have failed to control their disparate forces from within. Such a role would revive the concept of United Nations trusteeships, an instrument employed after World War II to administer former colonies until they were ready for independence.

Some diplomats say that Bosnia and Somalia might be early candidates for United Nations trusteeships, but no move in that direction has begun. And many experts worry about the precedent of the United Nations or any other instrument of the international community intervening where it may not be wanted, turning the United Nations into the new world's colonial power.

"We are at the point of claiming that the larger community has more rights of intervention," Senator Moynihan said. But he added: "I don't want a proposition that has the U.N. General Assembly deciding how we are handling our affairs in Elmira, N.Y."

The modes of possible future cooperation between the United States and the United Nations are only in the earliest stages of discussion.

For example, last summer, Secretary General Boutros-Ghali proposed a separate and permanent United Nations military force to intervene on behalf of the international community, either to prevent or stop ethnic conflicts within member states.

U.S. to Study Three Options

Mr. Boutros-Ghali's idea was quietly rebuffed by the Bush Administration, but the Clinton Administration may be more receptive. At his own confirmation hearings, Defense Secretary Les Aspin said the new administration would be studying three possibilities of some new kind of force with the United Nations.

In one option, he said there could be a permanent force assigned to the United Nations to intervene in other countries. In the second, various different countries might designate their own forces as available when needed by the United Nations.

The third option, he said, would be to establish a voluntary force for which Americans or individuals from any country could volunteer "like you could sign to join up in the French Foreign Legion." Mr. Aspin said he found all these ideas "interesting" and worth exploring.

On the other hand, Mr. Aspin ruled out allowing American troops to take part in a force under the command of the United Nations, saying such an arrangement would create "very serious and obvious constitutional problems" because the American units would be under the Secretary General.

New Institutions Suggested

Beyond the United Nations, some experts urge the creation

of new institutions altogether to deal with ethnic conflict. Such an institution might be an outgrowth of existing units, including the United Nations, the European Community, the North Atlantic Treaty Organization and the Conference on Security and Cooperation in Europe.

Mr. Christopher proposed consideration be given to setting up some kind of "international tribunal" to listen to claims on aggrieved minorities in countries. The tribunal's work would go beyond that of the International Court of Justice, which is confined to adjudicating claims between countries.

Mr. Moynihan asserts that the two dominant philosophical views of the century blinded officials into not recognizing that ethnic identity was going to be one of the most historical forces of the century.

The first philosophical view was Marxism, which predicted that ethnic identity would give way to conflict over ownership and production among economic classes. The second view was what Mr. Moynihan calls "the liberal expectancy"— the view of liberals from the time of Adam Smith in the 18th century that nations would get bigger for economic reasons and that ethnic factors would fade in significance.

"Both were wrong, and yet we have lived through the century seeing the world in these two perspectives," Mr. Moynihan said.

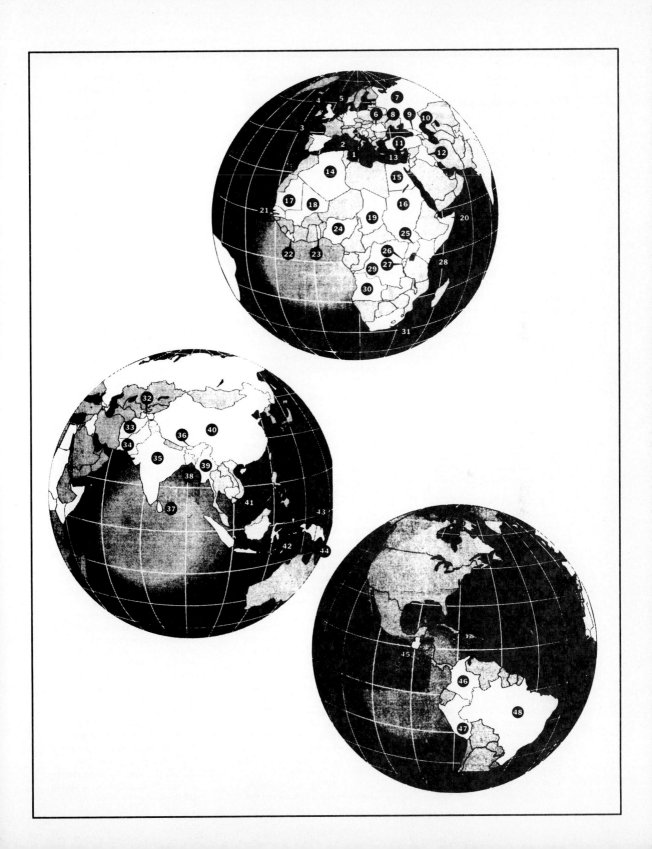

Europe

1. **Bosnia and Herzegovina**
Serbian forces have captured about 70 percent of the country and carried out an "ethnic cleansing" campaign that has expelled and killed Muslims and Croats and brought widespread condemnation. Tens of thousands of people have been estimated as killed—perhaps as many as 150,000 killed or missing—and 1.5 million uprooted from their homes.

2. **Croatia**   Serbian separatists control about a third of Croatia's territory. An estimated 25,000 have been killed since Croatia declared independence in 1991.

3. **Spain**   Nationalists saying they represent three million Basques seek an independent state on the border of Spain and France. Since 1968, 717 people have been killed in Spain and 49 in France.

4. **Britain**   The Protestant majority in Northern Ireland favors continued union with Britain while the Catholic minority wants to join with the rest of Ireland. More than 3,000 people have been killed in fighting between British troops, Protestant paramilitary groups and the Irish Republican Army since 1969.
   Britain has also seen a surge in attacks by whites on black and Asian immigrants.

5. **Germany**   An influx of 650,000 foreigners seeking asylum from Bulgaria, Romania, the Balkans and other areas has stirred anger in the last two years among right-wing groups. According to German authorities, right-wing and neo-Nazi groups carried out more than 2,000 attacks last year on asylum-seekers, resulting in 17 deaths and nearly 600 injuries.

6. **Romania**   Romania's ethnic Hungarians, mostly in Transylvania, want greater autonomy and the right to educate children in their language. There have been sporadic attacks on Gypsies.

7. **Russia**   Chechenya and Ingushetia have broken apart and seek greater autonomy within Russia. But Ingushetia and Northern Ossetia are fighting over

territory in clashes that have killed more than 300 people.

8. **Moldova**   Moldova's mainly Romanian population seeks economic, political and cultural ties with Romania. The Dniester region in eastern Moldova, where most of the population is of Russian and Ukrainian origin, declared independence in 1990, fearing that Moldova will unite with Romania. About 800 people have been killed and 4,000 others have been displaced by fighting.

9. **Georgia**   Abkhazia, dominated by Muslims, seeks independence or union with Russia. From 700 to 1,500 people are estimated to have been killed and 80,000 displaced in the fighting. Southern Ossetia, also dominated by Muslims, seeks union with Northern Ossetia, an autonomous republic in Russia. About 1,500 are estimated to have died in the fighting.

Middle East and North Africa

10. **Azerbaijan**   Troops from Muslim-dominated Azerbaijan, aided by Russian forces, are fighting to end a rebellion by Nagorno-Karabakh, an enclave within Azerbaijan populated largely by Christian Armenians, who favor independence or affiliation with Armenia. An estimated 3,000 people on both sides have been killed since 1989, and 350,000 Armenians and 500,000 Azerbaijanis have been displaced.
   In addition, Kurds in western Azerbaijan are demanding autonomy and have fought Azerbaijani forces.

11. **Turkey**   Kurdish separatists represented by the Marxist Kurdish Workers Party have sought a separate Kurdish state in fighting that has killed 2,500 since 1984.

12. **Iraq**   In the north, two major Kurdish parties rule in an enclave protected militarily by the United States and its allies. Several hundred have died in clashes with Iraqi forces since the 1991 Persian Gulf war. In the south, leaders of a rebellion by Shiite Muslims say that tens of thousands of Shiites have been killed by forces of the

Sunni-dominated Baghdad Government since the end of the Persian Gulf war.

13. **Israel**   The intifada, a popular uprising of Palestinians against Israeli occupation of the West Bank of the Jordan River and the Gaza Strip, erupted in 1987. About 1,000 Palestinians have been killed by Israeli soldiers, 500 have been killed by fellow Palestinians, and about 100 Israelis have been killed in Palestinian attacks.

14. **Algeria**   A revolt by Islamic militants has led to about 150 deaths in clashes with Government forces since the military canceled the second round of elections a year ago when Islamic parties were on the brink of winning a majority.

15. **Egypt**   More than 70 people have been killed in clashes between Islamic militants and Government security forces and in attacks by militants on foreigners and Coptic Christians.

16. **Sudan**   The Government, dominated by Arab Muslims from the north, is fighting a longstanding insurgency by black Christians and animists in South. Thousands have been reported killed and millions displaced.

Africa South of the Sahara

17. **Mauritania**   Government security forces under the Arab-dominated regime of Col. Maawiya Ould Sid Ahmed Taya have clashed with opposition groups angry over expulsions and oppression of the black minority.

18. **Mali**   A demand for sovereignty by ethnic Tuaregs, a light-skinned nomadic people living in both Mali and neighboring Niger, has led to fighting in both Mali and Niger.

19. **Chad**   President Idriss Déby, who ousted President Hissen Habré in 1990, has faced sporadic rebellions in the west and south of Chad. Some have reportedly involved clashes between Mr. Déby's Zakawa tribe and members of Mr. Habré's Gourane tribe.

20. **Somalia**   Clan fighting escalated into full-scale civil war in which 300,000 died and a million were

made homeless from war or starvation. An American-led military force has intervened and tried to establish stability.

21. **Senegal**   In Casamance, a coastal region mostly populated by the Diola tribe, there is opposition to Muslim domination in the government. Hundreds have been killed and thousands have been displaced in clashes with Government forces.

22. **Liberia**   At least 20,000 have been killed and hundreds of thousands have been uprooted in a civil war. Drawing support from the Gio and Mano ethnic groups, the guerrilla leader Charles Taylor controls most of the country. President Samuel K. Doe, from the Krahn ethnic group, was killed in 1990, and Monrovia is held by an interim government installed by West African nations as part of a regional peace effort.

23. **Togo**   Scores were killed last year as Government forces loyal to Togo's leader, Gen. Gnassingbé Eyadéma, of the Kabiye tribe, are battling opposition forces, including those from the rival Ewe tribe.

24. **Nigeria**   Nigeria, with about 200 ethnic groups, has many conflicts, but violence has been the sharpest in fighting between the Hausas, a predominantly Muslim group in the north, and the mostly Christian Yorubas in the south. Strife involving the Ibos in the east has been dormant in recent years.

25. **Uganda**   The army under President Yoweri K. Museveni, composed principally of members of the Baganda and Banyarwanda tribes, continues to wage sporadic warfare with northern rebels, mainly from the Acholi and Langi tribes.

26. **Rwanda**   Fighting is continuing between the Government, dominated by Hutu tribes, and an invading force led by the minority Tutsi tribe, despite an agreement between the Government and the rebels in July 1992. Tens of thousands have died in ethnic fighting in the last 30 years.

27. **Burundi**   Ethnic clashes between the majority ethnic group, the Hutus, and the minority

Tutsis have led to thousands of deaths in recent years.

28. **Kenya**   Clashes among tribes in 1991 and 1992 have reportedly killed 1,000 people and uprooted 50,000 and led to charges that the Government of President Daniel arap Moi was fomenting such conflict to discredit moves toward democracy.

29. **Zaire**   Thousands have died in the last year in a civil war between forces opposing and loyal to President Mobutu Sese Seko, and the fighting has ethnic overtones because various forces are from competing ethnic groups or tribes.

30. **Angola**   Renewed fighting between the Government and guerrilla forces led by Jonas Savimbi of the National Union for the Total Independence of Angola, or Unita, has left thousands dead and forced large numbers from their homes in the last few weeks. The struggle is ideological and political in nature, with ethnic overtones because Mr. Savimbi's strongest support comes from ethnic groups that have long felt disenfranchised by the leftist Luanda Government. There is also a violent secessionist movement in Cabinda, an oil-producing area that is geographically separated from the rest of Angola.

31. **South Africa**   Since 1984, about 15,000 have been killed in political violence related to a black insurrection against the white South African Government. About 3,000 were killed in 1992, many in clashes between Zulus and rival black groups.

Asia

32. **Tajikistan**   Tens of thousands of Tajik Muslims have been driven from their land by resurgent Communist armies seeking to suppress Islamic political power. More than 25,000 have been killed and 500,000 displaced since 1991.

33. **Afghanistan**   After the withdrawal of Soviet troops and the overthrow of the Soviet-installed leader, Najibullah, last year, the country has collapsed into civil

war among competing ethnic factions. The Hazars control central and western areas near Iran, the Pathans are largely in control in the east and the Tajiks largely control the north. Thousands are estimated to have been killed in recent fighting, and millions of Afghans remain in refugee camps in Pakistan and in Iran.

34. **Pakistan**   Thousands have died in conflicts between government forces and groups of secessionists and dissidents in Sindh and the Northwest Frontier Province. There has also been rioting in Karachi involving descendants of Muslims who emigrated from India at the time of partition with Pakistan in 1947.

35. **India**   Tensions between Hindus and Muslims exploded in December when Hindu militants razed a mosque in the northern state of Uttar Pradesh. Rioting that followed in many places across India led to 2,000 killings by official count, and many more by unofficial estimates. Killings by Muslims and Hindus continue. In Kashmir, 5,000 militants, civilians and Indian troops have been killed since a rebellion by the largely Muslim population began in 1990. An estimated 120,000 people, mostly Hindus, have fled Kashmir for other parts of India. In Punjab, about 20,000 Hindus and Sikhs are estimated to have been killed since a rebellion by Sikh militants erupted in 1982. In Assam, more than 200 have been reported killed as an insurgency by secessionists erupted in 1990. In Nagaland, insurgent Bodos have been fighting for a separate state; about 300 people have been killed.

36. **Bhutan**   A revolt by ethnic Nepalese against the Government and reprisals by Government forces have led to thousands of Nepalese fleeing the country in the last two years.

37. **Sri Lanka**   An insurgency by mostly Hindu Tamils in the north and east has been carried out against the Government, which is dominated by the mostly Buddhist Sinhalese. Since 1983, an estimated 28,000 people have been killed in the Tamil rebellion, and another

50,000 in the Government's crack-down on Sinhalese militants.

38. Bangladesh   A migration by members of the country's Muslim majority into the thinly populated Chittagong Hill Tracts region in the south has led to an insurgency by the area's Chakmas, a mainly Buddhist people, leaving hundreds dead and tens of thousands displaced.

39. Myanmar   In the last two years, more than 250,000 Muslims, charging harassment, have fled across the western border to Bangladesh. Hundreds are also believed to have died in clashes between Burmese soldiers and separatist Karen and other rebels along the Thai-Burmese border in the last two years.

40. China   Tibetans rebelled against Chinese rule in 1959, with an estimated 87,000 Tibetans killed. After an easing of Chinese rule, Beijing cracked down in 1987. Several dozen people are believed to have been killed in various incidents. In Xinjiang, China suppressed a rebellion among Muslims of Turkic descent in 1990 in which an estimated 50 people died.

41. Cambodia   Rebel factions signed a peace accord ending a 13-year civil war. A Supreme National Council made up of the rebel factions and the Cambodian Government is to advise the United Nations, which administers the country's affairs until a new government can be formed after elec-

tions this year. Various sides are constantly threatening to walk away from the agreement.

Khmer Rouge soldiers, who blame Vietnam for many of Cambodia's problems, have been carrying out attacks on 100,000 Vietnamese living in Cambodia.

42. Indonesia   A civil war broke out in East Timor in 1975 after Portugal withdrew, and Indonesia crushed the pro-independence rebellion. Human rights groups charge that 100,000 to 200,000 of the 600,000 mostly Roman Catholic East Timorese have died of starvation, disease or execution since Indonesia annexed the area.

A separatist movement also exists in northern Sumatra, where Indonesian forces are said by Amnesty International to have killed 2,000.

43. Papua New Giunea   Rebels on the island of Bougainville declared independence in 1990. The Papua New Guinea Government subdued the rebellion in 1991 after fighting in which 3,000 died.

44. Fiji   Violence erupted after the Indian-dominated Government was elected in 1987. The Government was overthrown and the current Government consolidates ethnic Fijian dominance.

Latin America

45. Guatemala   An essentially political conflict between the

Guatemalan Government and leftist guerrillas has had ethnic overtones because of the long history of repression of Indians in Guatemala. At least 43,000 Guatemalan refugees have fled into Mexico, but some are beginning to return.

46. Colombia   A group representing rights of Indians, Quintin Lamee, suspended an armed rebellion in 1991, but other Marxist groups claiming to represent peasants are continuing guerilla attacks on the government.

47. Peru   Since 1980, a Maoist guerrilla group known as Shining Path has waged war and won control of about a third of Peruvian territory, drawing support from largely Indian or mixed-race populations resisting the control of the mostly Hispanic elite in Lima. About 26,000 people have been killed in the war and an estimated 600,000 have fled their homes to other parts of the country. Thousands more have emigrated.

48. Brazil   Indian tribes in the Amazon region are pressing the Government in Brasélia to recognize their traditional homelands. In the northern Amazon state of Roraima, the federal Government is campaigning to expel gold miners from the lands of the Yanomami tribes.

QUESTIONS

1. U.S. Secretary of State Warren Christopher said that if ethnic groups can't learn to live with each other, the world could have 5,000 countries. What difference would it make to business if the number of countries increased substantially?

2. Examine the three options suggested for expanding the UN's dealings with ethnic conflicts and discuss how each may affect international differences.

3. The article lists areas of ethnic violence as of January 1993. What additional areas have experienced ethnic violence since then?

4. In addition to the violence in 48 nations listed in the article, what other non-violent separatist movements have existed in recent years?

Post Cold War Africa

With the exception of Somalia, South Africa, and Angola, events in Africa are rarely discussed. This article discusses the loss of interest in Africa on the part of industrial countries, some of the major problems Africa faces, and the promising trends. The political situation in nine African countries is summarized as an example of challenges facing African nations.

Relationship to text

◆◆ Chapter 2, pages 45–51, "The Political Environment," and 62–71, "Key Economic Issues in Industrial and Developing Countries"

◆◆ Chapter 6, page 211, "Direct Investment Motivation"

◆◆ Chapter 11, pages 309–310, "African Cooperation"

◆◆ Chapter 16, pages 578–582, "Influential Variables"

After studying the text, reading the article, and answering the questions, you should be able to:

◆◆ Explain why the cold war perpetuated an interest in Africa.

◆◆ Discuss why Africa was abandoned when the cold war ended.

◆◆ Identify some of the important problems and positive trends in African countries today.

Preview

◆ During the cold war, the superpowers courted African governments to protect their own interests and curb the influence of opposing powers.

◆ In recent years, nations have provided positive assistance to Africa's crises.

◆ Foreign direct investment to Africa has been declining, but activity has increased to Latin American and Asian countries.

◆ The AIDS epidemic has ravaged Africa; estimates indicate that 7.5 million African adults are infected.

◆ The number of democratic elections and economic liberalization programs are increasing.

Africa: From the Cold War to Cold Shoulders

Having been carved up and colonized by European powers and turned into pawns, knights and rooks on a cold war chessboard by the superpowers, Africa now faces a devastating new problem: indifference.

Writing in the current issue of *Foreign Affairs Quarterly*, Marguerite Michaels, a fellow at the Council on Foreign Relations, noted that the disintegration of the Soviet Union "set America free to pursue its own interests in Africa—and it found that it did not have any."

It is a harsh assessment. But with the end of the cold war, Africa's strategic importance to the West has declined. With shrinking per capita income hampering the development of markets for Western goods, political instability and a poorly educated work force making investment unattractive, and declining demand in the West for many of the continent's raw materials like copper and cobalt, Africa's economic significance has been reduced. Humanitarian impulses may keep the West engaged but, as has been shown by Ethiopia and Somalia, those impulses seem to be triggered only when countries have slid into chaos and famine.

Evidence of the world's fatigue with the unremitting problems of Africa or fumbling when it has become engaged are both real and symbolic. The United Nations failed to disarm both sides in the Angolan conflict before holding elections there in September and then watched helplessly as the apparent loser, Jonas Savimbi, took up arms after the results were in. In Mozambique, both sides in a long civil war seem committed to a peace settlement, but the United Nations has yet to deploy a peacekeeping force to insure that the agreement sticks. Zaire's autocratic President, Mobutu Sese Seko, rewarded handsomely by the United States during the cold war for his staunch anti-communism, so far has easily resisted pressure to democratize from the Americans as well as from Belgium, the former colonial power, and France. His country, facing secessionist pressures and growing lawlessness by unpaid soldiers, is slouching toward anarchy.

Meanwhile, the State Department, focusing on Eastern Europe and the former Soviet Union, has cut 70 positions from its Bureau of African Affairs and closed down consulates or embassies in Kenya, Cameroon, Nigeria and the Comoro Islands. The Agency for International Development has slashed staff and programs serving Africa, and only the 11th-hour intervention of the Congressional Black Caucus kept the House Foreign Affairs Committee from merging its Africa subcommittee with the panel handling Latin America. Though recent Administrations have spoken of the continent's importance, no President has set foot in sub-Saharan Africa since Jimmy Carter in 1978.

Diminishing Interest

"I'm not nostalgic about the cold war," Salim A. Salim, Secretary General of the Organization of African Unity, said during a speech last week in Washington. "I am very happy the cold is over. What I am saying is that there is diminishing interest in the issues of real human concern."

The issues are manifold. Though aid has increased dramatically since the mid-1980's, African countries remain saddled with debt and there is virtually no new commercial lending. While direct private investment has tripled in Latin America and increased fivefold in East Asia since 1985, it has declined in Africa. AIDS continues to ravage Africa; the World Health Organization reports that 7.5 million of the 12 million adults worldwide infected with the H.I.V. virus are African. And from the Horn of Africa to the bulge to central and southern Africa, wars, chaos and ethnic conflict seem all too much the order of the day.

But to view Africa as nothing but a bleak landscape is to miss the blossoms among the weeds. "If you look from one week to the next, the cup is more empty than full," said a State Department official. "But if you look over the last few years, the overall trend is in the right direction. The number of democratic elections is going up. The number of economic liberalization programs is going up."

Peace is holding in Mozambique and in Namibia, which won independence in 1990 after decades of rule by South Africa in defiance of the United Nations. Kenya, Zambia, Ethiopia, Mali and Benin are inching, or in some places running, toward multiparty democracy after decades of one-party rule or military dictatorship. (The democratically elected Zambian Government's roundup of opponents last week under state of emergency illustrated the fragility of the trend in some places.) Under prodding by the World Bank, 26 countries have restructured their economies and are expanding their trade. South Africa is moving toward multiracial democracy. If successful, it could turn from a pariah into a democratic example for the multi-ethnic nations of black Africa, and become a trading partner and source of capital for the rest of southern Africa.

Perhaps the most significant development is the willingness of Africans to admit their own past mistakes—to stop placing the blame for the continent's underdevelopment entirely on the West and the legacy of colonialism, and instead condemn gross abuses by incompetent or venal leaders.

In addition, African leaders are now willing to contribute troops to help bring about peace, as demonstrated most recently in Somalia. The shift in African attitudes first became evident in 1990, when West African states concluded that if they didn't do something about the strife in Liberia to insure the stability of their region, no one else would; a Nigerian-led peace force intervened.

In the past, the principle of non-intervention in the internal affairs of other African countries, enshrined in the charter of the Organization of African Unity, gave leaders cover for inaction even in the face of blatant abuses by rulers like Idi Amin of Uganda.

"We allowed the violations of human rights," Mr. Salim said. "We allowed the dehumanization of our people and used the charter as a scapegoat."

Big Brushfires, Dire Landscape

Angola

Peace talks between the Government and the National Union for the Total Independence of Angola, or Unita, the rebel group led by Jonas Savimbi, broke down last week, the latest failed effort to end the 17-year civil war. Elections were held last September under 1991 peace accords brokered by the superpowers. But Mr. Savimbi, once backed by the United States, balked at results giving victory to President Jose Eduardo dos Santos. Health conditions in the country are said to have deteriorated sharply as a result of the war.

Liberia

A three-sided conflict continues. The participants: the National Patriotic Front of Liberia, a rebel group that helped overthrow the dictator Samuel K. Doe in 1990; a rival guerrilla group made up of former soldiers in Mr. Doe's army and members of his tribe, the Krahn; and a peacekeeping force sent by West African countries. It is estimated that 25,000 Liberians—about 1 percent of the population—have been killed.

Mozambique

The country is on the mend from a 16-year civil war and famine. A peace agreement between the Government and the guerrilla group Renamo has held since its signing in October. But diplomats fear that unless the United Nations overcomes delays in deploying a 7,500-member peace force, the peace could fall apart.

Rwanda

Civil war rages between the Tutsi, the former ruling class, and the Hutus, who overthrew them in 1973. The Tutsi, largely driven into exile, now seek to return. The conflict is made worse by demographic factors; Rwanda is Africa's most densely populated country and has its highest birth rate.

Somalia

The United States, which in December mounted an international military effort to insure relief deliveries, has been gradually withdrawing most of its forces as the United Nations prepares to assume control of the operation this spring. Starvation has eased, but disarmament efforts have met with mixed success and little has been done to rebuild centralized authority.

Sudan

Relief agencies warn of a disaster on a scale of that seen in Somalia before the American-led intervention. As in Somalia, the main culprit is not drought but armed conflict. Rebels in the mostly Christian and animist south have been fighting the Muslim-dominated Government in Khartoum since 1983. Both sides have routinely hampered relief efforts, and the Government has indiscriminately bombed southern villages. Since 1991, the guerrillas' ranks have splintered, and recent fighting among them has added to the bloodshed.

Togo

More than 230,000 refugees have fled to Benin and Ghana since fighting erupted in Lomé, the Togolese capital, in January. Togo has had a supposedly transitional Government intended to pave the way for democracy after 23 years of dic-

tatorial rule by President Gnassingbe Eyadema. But Mr. Eyadema has resisted calls to give up power.

Uganda

Peaceful after years of violence under the Governments of Idi Amin and Milton Obote, Uganda is being ravaged by AIDS. It is estimated that 9 percent of Uganda's 16.7 million people are infected.

Zaire

Diplomats warn of economic and political collapse as President Mobutu Sese Seko resists Western demands that he share power with his Prime Minister, Etienne Tshisekedi, who is supposed to be steering the country to democracy. Soldiers loyal to Mr. Mobutu who have gone unpaid appear increasingly bent on lawlessness.

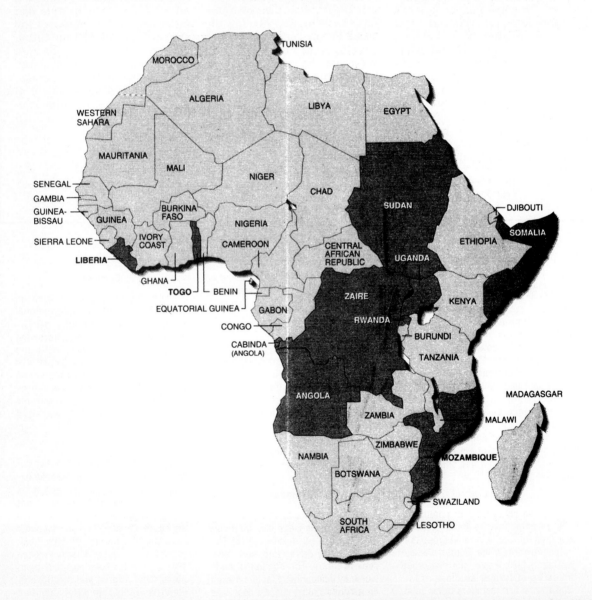

QUESTIONS

1. Why has Africa's economic significance been reduced since the end of the cold war?

2. What has been the attitude of the U.S. Government toward Africa, as Eastern Europe and the former Soviet Union have accepted Western influence?

3. What has happened to capital inflows into Africa in recent years?

4. Describe some of the political trends that have been moving in a positive direction.

ARTICLE 6

OUTLOOK IMPROVING FOR MNE OPERATIONS IN LATIN AMERICA

Most Latin American economies fared poorly in the 1980s, and multinational firms were disinterested. However, MNEs, especially from the United States, have recently shifted their attention to Latin America. A combination of actual and projected economic performance (along with a more welcoming attitude toward foreign firms) has made Latin America more attractive.

Relationship to text

◆◆ Chapter 1, pages 18–21, "Influences on Trade and Investment Patterns"

◆◆ Chapter 2, pages 62–71, "Key Economic Issues in Industrial and Developing Countries"

◆◆ Chapter 11, pages 403–406, "Latin American Cooperation"

◆◆ Chapter 13, pages 468–471, "Needs and Alternatives for Fulfillment"

◆◆ Chapter 16, pages 578–588, "Influential Variables"

After studying the text, reading the article, and answering the questions, you should be able to:

◆◆ Describe recent policy changes in Latin America that have improved the region's attractiveness to foreign investors.

◆◆ Understand how freer trade among Latin American countries changes the methods by which foreign firms organize their operations to serve Latin American markets.

◆◆ Outline the operational forms used by foreign firms in Latin America and contrast these forms with earlier periods.

Preview

◆ U.S. trade with and direct investment to Latin America have recently increased substantially.

◆ Multinational enterprises have been favorably influenced by changes in economic policies of Latin American governments, such as privatization programs, anti-inflationary measures, and freer trade policies.

◆ Latin America has recently encouraged foreign ownership and has been willing to negotiate on policies of interest to foreign firms.

Multinationals Step Lively to the Free-Trade Bossa Nova

As Markets Open Up, U.S. Companies Scurry to Revamp and Regionalize Their Latin Operations

The top brass of 20 big multinational companies shifted uneasily in their seats around the conference table in the Economy Ministry's stark, modern meeting salon. They were waiting for their regular luncheon with Economy Minister Marcélio Marques Moreira, whose no-nonsense style had always inspired confidence. The Minister was late—and Brasélia was rife with rumors of an impending political shakeup by President Fernando Collor de Mello.

When Marques Moreira finally walked in, he stunned the group with the news that Collor had asked his entire Cabinet to resign. Then, after a pause, he brought the executives to their feet in a standing ovation with the laconic addendum: "The President asked me to stay on the job."

Partly, the applause was in recognition of Marques Moreira's success so far in moving Brazil toward a more stable, free-market economy after years of inflationary lurches and statist controls. It also underscored the unabashed welcome that U.S. companies now sense in Brazil—and in most of Latin America—after decades of contradictory policies. Over the years, Brazil has attracted big investments by companies such as General Motors Corp. and Volkswagen, but Brasélia has also hobbled carmakers and other manufacturers with oppressive regulation inspired by bouts of nationalism. One example was Brazil's rules barring foreign companies from the personal computer business.

No Flag

That kind of heavy-handed regulation is being eased in many countries. Argentine President Carlos Menem has ended discrimination against foreign companies, insisting that "capital carries no flag." And in Brazil, the blue-chip Foreign Investors' Group meets every two or three months with Marques Moreira to discuss ways of improving the business climate. Representatives of U.S. companies include the heads of Brazilian subsidiaries of IBM, Cargill, and American Express. "We don't get together with the Minister just to shoot the breeze," says Séo Paulo publisher Christopher Lund, a former president of the American Chamber of Commerce for Brazil, who coordinates the group. "We make actual progress" on issues—such as a tax cut on remitted profits that the group suggested and the government adopted.

Across Latin America, the market opening is allowing multinational companies to draw a hodgepodge of high-cost operations, originally set up to do business in protected markets, into their worldwide strategies. That could lift their profits and strengthen their hand against global competitors—particularly the Japanese. With few major manufacturing investments in Latin America, Japanese companies aren't so well positioned to cash in on the region's recovery. For U.S. companies, it all adds up to "the biggest opportunity in Latin America in 50 years," says Zeke Wimert, president of software maker Oracle Corp.'s Brazilian subsidiary.

American investors, and Europeans as well, are breaking through many once-sensitive cultural barriers. Pizza Hut International would once have been seen as a Yanqui assault on local cuisine, yet it now has 100 franchises from Chile to Mexico and aims for 500. Hungry for a taste of European style, Latin Americans are also flocking to Benetton Group's 316 stores in 10 countries. Latins are also displaying a more welcoming attitude toward foreign investment in politically sensitive businesses, including petroleum and mining.

To be sure, Americans are testing the new order more cautiously in South America than in next-door Mexico. U.S. exports to the region are up (chart), but Americans are not laying out up to $700 million a crack for brand-new plants in the

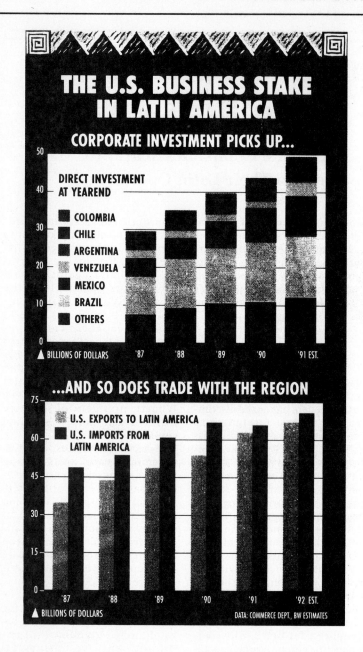

THE U.S. BUSINESS STAKE IN LATIN AMERICA

CORPORATE INVESTMENT PICKS UP...

DIRECT INVESTMENT AT YEAREND

■ COLOMBIA
■ CHILE
■ ARGENTINA
■ VENEZUELA
■ MEXICO
■ BRAZIL
■ OTHERS

▲ BILLIONS OF DOLLARS   '87 '88 '89 '90 '91 EST.

...AND SO DOES TRADE WITH THE REGION

U.S. EXPORTS TO LATIN AMERICA
U.S. IMPORTS FROM LATIN AMERICA

▲ BILLIONS OF DOLLARS   '87 '88 '89 '90 '91 '92 EST.

DATA: COMMERCE DEPT., BW ESTIMATES

ing forces in strategic alliances with local companies

Of course, such transactions are easy to dream up in corporate headquarters. Carrying them out on the ground is still a rough job. Executives in Brazil must ship through ports that charge steep prices for abominable service. And try juggling wildly different inflation rates while consolidating business across borders

Copycat Plants

Despite these obstacles, companies are plowing ahead. Consider Xerox do Brasil. As Brazilian tariffs fall, it has lowered costs drastically by replacing local materials and components with cheaper imports. In years past, the government required Xerox to make copiers with up to 90% local content. Xerox has slashed costs by 30% by lowering national content from 90% to 40%. That's a competitive gain for Xerox worldwide, since the Brazilian company exports components to Xerox plants in other countries. But the market opening is heating up competition in Brazil: In less than two years, Xerox' share of the Brazilian market dropped from 96% to 80%.

For nearly a half-century, U.S. companies organized their Latin American operations for a patchwork of small national markets, separated by protectionist walls. For some, that meant building copycat plants in each of a dozen countries. Now, there are opportunities for rationalizing operations by better matching of markets and manufacturing capacity, and in some cases, by shutting down unneeded plants.

Dow Chemical Co., for example, has factories making latex and emulsions in both Brazil and Argentina. In the past, it would have had to expand the plants

rest of Latin America as they have in Mexico.

To get ready for that day, U.S. multinationals are rapidly reshaping their operations in the region. The aim is to prepare once-sheltered subsidiaries for global competition

as trade barriers fall. These units are racing to modernize, cut costs, and raise product quality. They also are linking operations across national borders to take advantage of lowered trade barriers. In some cases, they are join-

separately to meet demand in each market. Now, Dow is trading products between Brazil and Argentina and won't expand either facility until the capacity of both has been used up. It is also swapping products between plants in Venezuela and Colombia. "We cannot afford any more to build for one market and pretend it's going to be protected from competition," says Dow Venezuela President Frederico Montaner.

While some companies are streamlining, others are retooling to make their operations more competitive. Cummins Engine Co.'s Brazilian subsidiary makes diesel engines and supplies components to Cummins plants in other countries. To compensate for a sharp drop in local sales because of Brazil's recession, Cummins plans to spend $40 million to expand exports. One target is Argentina, a partner in Mercosur—the free-trade bloc set up by Argentina, Brazil, Paraguay, and Uruguay.

General Electric Co., meanwhile, is pushing hard to raise its Latin American productivity to world levels. In Brazil, GE makes capital goods such as railroad locomotives and motors along with other products from lamps to plastics. While the company is expanding headlong in Mexico, notably in joint ventures making gas ranges and plastics, in South America "we are investing in productivity and quality," says Kurt J. Meier, chairman of São Paulo-based General Electric do Brasil. And GE is demanding improved performance by local suppliers as well. "We give [a supplier] a reasonable time to get down to world costs," Meier says. "If not, we import."

Crane Selling

To keep its locomotive business alive, though, GE is putting it into a 50-50 joint venture with Villares Group, a Brazilian conglomerate that was a GE rival till now. Both have been battered by the drop in Brazil's appetite for heavy capital goods in the past five years. "We have to rationalize [production] to maintain the technology within the country," Meier says. To do so, GE and Villares are spending $90 million to move Villares' equipment for building locomotives, electric motors, and overhead cranes to a joint facility at GE's Campinas plant near São Paulo.

By contrast, IBM recently set up a personal-computer joint venture with Villares for a very different motive: to get a fast start in the rapidly expanding PC business, which Brazil is opening to foreigners on Oct. 28. To survive, Brazilian computer companies are looking to team up with U.S. partners such as IBM and Hewlett-Packard Co. Under the old law, IBM Brasil was allowed to build mainframes. Now, with the end of Brazil's restrictions, it is free to start manufacturing PCs or import them on its own. Instead, IBM has formed a joint venture with Villares, formerly an IBM distributor, to import work stations, taking advantage of Villares' established customer base. IBM also has deals with three other Brazilian companies to assemble computers and provide services.

For U.S. oil and mining companies, what's crucial in Latin America's new free-market climate is not the lowering of trade barriers. It is the about-face from heavy government regulation and frequent hostility against foreign investors. In mineral-rich Peru, for example, President Alberto K. Fujimori plans to privatize all state-owned companies, including mines expropriated from U.S. companies decades ago. First Boston Corp. and Chase Manhattan Corp. are helping organize the sell-off of formerly American-owned properties.

In oil, the shift in attitude is most notable in Argentina, which is selling off once-protected production rights and plans to privatize the national oil company, YPF. But the rigid ban against any foreign role in exploration and production is weakening in oil-rich Venezuela, too. The change in sentiment is being speeded by the cash squeeze on the national oil company, PDVSA, which is strapped for money to carry out expansion plans.

No Smooth Ride

A sign of the times is the return to Venezuela of Exxon, which lost 1 million barrels per day of oil production when its operations were nationalized in 1975. It has reopened a Caracas office, Exxon Services Venezuela Inc., to pursue ventures such as a proposal, with partners, to build a $20 billion liquefied natural gas plant. Within a decade, Exxon Vice-President Bill Baisley predicts, "you're going to see a major part of the Venezuelan oil industry be operated under joint-venture agreements."

Despite the free-market reforms, U.S. executives hardly expect a smooth ride in Latin America. While the broad move toward private enterprise is unlikely to reverse, governments will still come and go, and rules can change. To be an investor in Latin America, says Brian Hill, head of Cargill Inc.'s Brazilian operations, "you have to be comfortable with the swings."

The irony is that in this region, Americans may be better at riding out the swings than their Japanese competitors because they have deeper roots. GE set up its first business in Mexico in 1896, and Gillette Co.

started manufacturing in Brazil in 1931. Europeans, though less numerous, are also well entrenched. But the inevitable Latin ups and downs, while frustrating to all foreigners, have been a particular turnoff to the cautious Japanese. With few exceptions, they have been reluctant to make major commitments in manufacturing.

As a result, Americans are strengthening their stake in rapidly growing markets where their toughest worldwide rival is not well represented. The flow of profits and the economies of scale from Latin America are likely to reinforce U.S. multinationals' global competitive strength. So, while the region's economic revival is restoring hope for Latin Americans after a decade of stagnation, for U.S. companies competing worldwide it is also very good news.

Questions

1. How would you rate opportunities for business in Latin America in the next few years compared to opportunities in other parts of the world?

2. Recently Latin American countries have welcomed foreign investment; however, historically there have been periods of welcome followed by restrictions and nationalizations. Do you believe the current attitudes are more permanent? What factors might influence a change in attitude?

3. What advantages might U.S. firms have over firms from Europe or Japan in tapping business opportunities in Latin America?

4. How have recent Latin American trade policies affected companies' decisions to follow multidomestic versus global operating strategies?

ARTICLE 7

ECONOMIC GROWTH IN ASIA

Speculation exists that in 25 years, the combined GNP of Asia will be larger than that of Europe and twice that of the United States. This estimate implies greater political and economic strength for Asian countries, if they can act in a homogeneous manner. However, complete Asian dominance is not totally certain.

Relationship to text

◆◆ Chapter 2, pages 45–51, "The Political Environment," and pages 62–71, "Key Economic Issues in Industrial and Developing Countries"

◆◆ Chapter 6, page 211, "Direct Investment Motivation"

◆◆ Chapter 11, pages 408–409, "Asian Cooperation"

◆◆ Chapter 16, pages 578–582, "Influential Variables"

After studying the text, reading the article, and answering the questions, you should be able to:

◆◆ Discuss why many Asians feel East Asia will eventually overtake Europe and North America economically.

◆◆ Identify ways in which this balance of economic power could affect interaction between Asia and the West.

◆◆ Evaluate the accuracy of the following statement: "The balance of power will shift from West to East."

◆◆ Examine the impact of this shift on U.S. firms.

Preview

◆ Various Asian experts estimate that within the near future, Asia will surpass Europe and North America as the most important economic region in the world.

◆ Greater economic power should further Asia's influence in world councils on human rights, economic growth, the environment, and protectionist responses to trade.

◆ Several experts argued that Asians overstate the decline of the West, specifically North America.

Indicators Point to Coming Asian Century

Economic Dominance May Arrive in about 25 Years

Sometime early in the next century, Asia will eclipse North America as the world's most powerful region.

That dramatic idea is gaining considerable popularity in Asia these days, however much some may dispute it.

One of its most enthusiastic advocates is George Yeo, Singapore's Minister of information. The 38-year-old Mr. Yeo not only believes that Asia is likely soon to be the world's dominant region economically, but that this economic dominance will inevitably translate into political and cultural power as well, making Asia truly the world's leader.

"In 25 years, the combined GNP of East Asia will be larger than all of Europe's and twice that of the U.S.," Mr. Yeo declared in a speech in Davos, Switzerland, in February. GNP, or gross national product, is the total value of goods and services produced in a country. "The unfolding East Asian renaissance will challenge and transform all cultures in the world and change the way man looks at himself."

It's a thesis of obvious relevance to anyone interested in Asia's world role. For if Asia's role really is to be No. 1, the implication would be profound. Mr. Yeo cites the mass media as an example of the epochal power shift he thinks lies ahead. "The Western domination of the global media will be contested," he predicted in his Davos speech.

But clearly the implications of a power shift wouldn't stop there. Asian spokesmen would have a bigger say in world councils. Asian viewpoints on human rights, economic growth and the environment would command more of a hearing in the world marketplace of ideas. Western nations, and the U.S. in particular, would no longer be free to push Asia around, imposing sanctions and erecting protectionist barriers willy-nilly. Instead, Asia might do a little pushing around of its own.

Wishful thinking? Perhaps. But it's easy to understand why some Asians have such an optimistic view of Asia's prospects. The immediate reasons include China's economic boom and the resilience of economic growth throughout the region, even during a period of U.S. and European recessions. No longer does Asia catch a cold when America sneezes. In fact, many Asians subscribe to the view that the U.S. is irreversibly in decline.

The deeper, underlying reasons are Asia's three billion people and the growing confidence in the region that Asia knows how to put these multitudes to work productively.

In the past, having more than half of the earth's population on less than a third of the earth's available land seemed like an obstacle to Asia's modernization. But in the past generation, one densely populated Asian country after another has followed Japan down the road of rapid economic development and rapid labor-productivity growth, and now

China seems headed down that road as well.

With a population 10 times that of North America and six times that of Europe, and with faster growth rates than either North America or Europe, Asia at some point would inevitably overtake the other two regions economically, in total output if not in per-capita terms. And that point may be coming sooner than perhaps most Americans and Europeans realize.

Including Japan, Asia's economic output could overtake North America's as early as 1996, predicts David O'Rear, senior consultant and regional economist at the Economist Intelligence Unit in Hong Kong. Excluding Japan, Mr. O'Rear sees Asia overtaking North America in 2018 and the European Community in 2022.

Enzio von Pfeil, chief regional economist at S.G. Warburg Securities (Far East) Ltd. in Hong Kong, sees Asia minus Japan overtaking the U.S. in 2015 and the EC in 2020. Looking out over a longer period, some people in the region see an even bigger economic role for Asia.

Gus Hooke, an Australian economist, predicts that by 2050 Asia excluding Japan will account for 57% of the world's economy. The 24 industrialized countries that make up the Organization for Economic Cooperation and Development, including the U.S., Japan, and most of Europe, will account for only 12%, Mr. Hooks predicts. In 1990, by contrast, the OECD countries accounted for 74% of the world's economy, while Asia had only 9%.

Asian Economies
1991 Gross National Product

Country	GNP (In millions of U.S. dollars)	GNP (Per capita)
Japan	$3,337,191	$26,920
China	424,012	370
South Korea	274,464	6,340
Taiwan	179,763	8,788
Indonesia	111,409	610
Thailand	89,548	1,580
Philippines	46,138	740
Malaysia	45,787	2,490
Singapore	39,249	12,890

Sources: World Bank, China External Trade Development Council (Taiwan)

The logical leap from that kind of economic dominance to political and cultural power is practically effortless. The U.S. today is able to extract trade concessions and promises of human rights improvements from Asian nations at least in part because all of them covet access to the huge, rich U.S. market. In the future, the huge, rich markets will be in Asia.

Or so goes the Asia-as-No.1 thesis. But does the thesis hold water? Here are some of the places critics see leaks:

- Straight-line projections into the distant future are inherently risky. Consider the non-implausible scenario that U.S. economy experiences a spurt of real recovery next year, while China's juggernaut stumbles on infrastructure bottlenecks and inflation. Redoing the forecast with new growth rates to take that reversal of fortunes into account, Asia might not overtake the other two regions

until 2025 or 2030. The farther out the date, the greater the likelihood that unexpected intervening events render the whole exercise irrelevant. Let China suffer a recession lasting two or three years and people might be rethinking the whole idea.

- Don't forget the competition. North America and Europe may have smaller populations, but they start from a much higher base of wealth and technology, and their growth rates might not stagnate forever. The U.S. has its problems, but many Asians seem to have an overly pessimistic view of its prospects.

- Asia isn't one place. Many of those celebrating Asia's rise come from smaller countries in the region. In China, they don't talk about Asia as No. 1; they talk about China as the next superpower. Before basking in the glow of China's modernization, other Asians must ponder whether they can form a united front with this superpower, or whether China's rise to superpower status won't inevitably trigger intra-Asian conflicts that will prevent Asia from making the most of its advantages. Even assuming no conflicts, will Asia be one big market, or many? The less unified it is, the less ability it has to exert influence in the world.

- Economics isn't everything. That's worth stressing because so many Asians see Japan as the paradigm for their future, big on financial and technological muscle, light on military might. But the Japan formula only works because of Japan's relationship with the U.S., a re-

lationship that benefits Japan enormously at the same time it detracts from Japan's ability to be No. 1.

- The relationship between economic power on the one hand and political and cultural power on the other is at best indirect. Britain's economy has been in relative decline for a century, while Japan's has soared to the No.2 position in the world. But that does not mean Japan projects more political or cultural power than Britain. National power can help promote the spread of a nation's popular culture to be sure, but a powerful idea can have a life of its own regardless of the nationality of its originator, and vice versa. Gandhi's nonviolent resistance gained adherents around the world even though India was hardly a bastion of economic strength. Singapore is a tiny island republic, but its intellectuals' trenchant articles appear on op-ed pages around the world.

- Beware the magic of statistics. The time frame for Asia overtaking the other two regions depends in part on how big Asia's economy and in particular China's economy, is now. If China's per-capita gross domestic product is $370 per year, as official statistics indicate, then China's overall output is less than a tenth of that of the U.S. If the figure is $1,950 a year, as a World Bank report concluded by using "regression analysis" instead of the reported data, China's output now is almost half that of the U.S.

At some point Asia logically ought to have a bigger economy

than Europe and America. But, while having the highest total economic output will boost Asia's pride, catching up with the rest of the world in per-capita terms will take much longer. For the happiness of Asia's citizens, if not the region's ability to project power, it's the latter that matters most.

WALL STREET JOURNAL: Urban C. Lehner, "Indicators Point to Coming Asian Century," May 17, 1993, p. A 12. Reprinted by permission of *The Wall Street Journal*, © 1993 Dow Jones & Co., Inc. All Rights Reserved Worldwide.

QUESTIONS

1. What are the major reasons why Asia may overtake Europe and North America economically within the near future?

2. In what ways could Asia's economic power result in greater influence? Why?

3. What is the difference in economic power between the OECD and Asia minus Japan now, and what may it be by the year 2050?

4. If Asia's political and economic power grows as predicted by the Asian experts, how may it affect U.S. firms?

5. What are some of the problems with the assumptions behind future Asian dominance?

THE URUGUAY ROUND CONTINUES

Since the Uruguay Round of GATT negotiations began in 1986, serious problems have kept the round from being concluded. The U.S. opposition to the European Community's position on farm subsidies was partially resolved in the fall of 1992. Although negotiations were started again, it is difficult to predict how a resolution will be attained with a more protectionist U.S. administration and a worldwide recession that emphasizes protectionism versus flexibility.

Relation to text

◆◆ Chapter 5, pages 186–189, "The Role of GATT"

After studying the text, reading the article, and answering the questions, you should be able to:

◆◆ Identify the underlying position of the new United States administration toward trade negotiations.

◆◆ Discuss the major issues and obstacles involved in reaching a conclusion to current GATT negotiations.

◆◆ Highlight the specific aims of the renewed discussions in the GATT round.

◆◆ Explain why the United States is pushing for a new enforcement mechanism for GATT.

Preview

◆ President Clinton and the new administration appear to be concerned about fair trade and safeguards for workers.

◆ The Uruguay Round has been breaking through tough non-tariff barriers, as well as reducing tariffs.

◆ A major stumbling block in negotiations has been concern in non-EC countries about farm subsidies in the EC and the refusal of French farmers to see those subsidies cut.

◆ GATT is not doing a good job of resolving disputes.

The GATT Struggle Continues

In 1824 Thomas Babington Macaulay, the British historian, declared that free trade is one of the greatest blessings that a government can confer on a people. "Unfortunately," he added, "it is in almost every country unpopular."

This unpopularity can be found in the U.S. today, at least among certain groups. President Clinton has hedged his commitment to the North American Free Trade Agreement, for example, by calling for "fair trade" rules and "safeguards for our workers." Another test of his commitment to free trade will be his stance toward the General Agreement on Tariffs and Trade.

For six long years, the 108 nations that signed GATT have been struggling to make important additions to the agreement, additions that most members think would be to everyone's advantage. Optimists think the talks, which began in 1986 at the pleasant resort of Punto del Este, Uruguay, are still on track. Pessimists worry about several proposals that are more than somewhat unpopular.

GATT's chief aim, when it was founded in 1947, was to reduce tariffs, and in this area its achievements have been considerable. So, at Punto del Este, the U.S. decided to aim for more difficult targets. The talks are supposed to reduce nontariff barriers and strengthen international rules affecting general market access, agriculture, services, the textiles trade, intellectual property rights, dispute settlements, safeguards and enforcement measures under GATT.

A major obstacle from the start of the talks has been U.S. opposition to European Community farm subsidies—and the EC's refusal to change them. Finally, in November, compromises were reached, at least temporarily heading off what looked like a trade war. The U.S. and other non-EC farm exporters wanted something close to elimination of the subsidies, and they aren't fully satisfied with the much more modest cuts that were made. The French farmers, for their part, aren't happy that any cuts were made. French elections are coming up this month and the French government has threatened to veto the Uruguay package.

The compromises, however, made it possible for negotiations to proceed. Among the specific aims are reform of quota-blighted trade in textiles and garments, new rules for patents and copyrights, and the first real effort to implement free trade in services. One of the major changes some Americans would like to see is a new enforcement mechanism. GATT's existing mechanism ruled against the EC farm subsidies many months ago. But the U.S. and other farm exporters then could only sit down and talk over the situation—or move toward a trade war.

This wasn't the way things were supposed to work. At the talks in Geneva in 1946, GATT planners envisioned something called the International Trade Organization. The planners were smart enough to know that disputes would arise, and the ITO was supposed to administer any trade rules.

It seemed like a good idea. But the proposal went to the U.S. Congress, and the lawmakers shot it down. The post-World War II period was an era when international organizations were being created all over the place. Many Americans felt there were too many of them with too much power. So the ITO never came into existence.

Trade disputes, of course, didn't disappear. When troubles such as the EC farm subsidies arose, the various parties were supposed to sit down and talk things over. The ringmaster for all this talk was supposed to be Arthur Dunkel, the director general of GATT. Mr. Dunkel is a French Swiss and an able man. But there are some GATT-watchers who think he could have done more to keep the negotiations on track.

Mr. Dunkel can claim some achievements, notably in persuading the EC to agree to the farm subsidy compromise. But some of Mr. Dunkel's critics in the U.S. and elsewhere think he's not tough enough. In mid-December, for instance, he reopened negotiations on several matters on which everyone had implicitly agreed. There's no indication why he did this, especially since he had just been urging everyone to keep amendments to a minimum.

The Americans have been making trouble, too. Proposals have been made to create something like the

ITO. American environmentalists are afraid some such fully fledged organization would use its powers to discourage laws designed to protect the environment. U. S. industrial groups want stronger powers to slap anti-dumping duties on foreign exporters. And somewhat to the surprise of foreign negotiators, the Americans want stronger protection for intellectual property. Many foreign negotiators feel that major gains already have been made in this area.

There's no way to tell what will happen now that the trade talks are in the Clinton administration's hands. Sir Leon Brittan, the EC commissioner for external economic affairs, so far sees no change in the new administration's approach to the talks. Mickey Kantor, Mr. Clinton's trade representative, speaks modestly of his lack of experience in trade matters. But he made his professional reputation as a tough negotiator, and the talks need some toughness if they are ever to succeed.

QUESTIONS

1. Why is the Clinton administration concerned with fair trade and safeguards for workers, and how could these issues affect the current GATT negotiations?

2. What are some of the nontariff barriers being debated in the Uruguay round?

3. Why is agriculture such an important issue in the GATT round?

4. Why isn't the U.S. pleased with the current director general of GATT?

ARTICLE 9

IMPLEMENTING THE EC SINGLE MARKET

On January 1, 1993, the Single Internal Market came into effect in the European Community. A major concern of companies from non-EC countries is the consequence of this new Single Market. This article discusses the status of the Single Market, how the new regulations might affect non-EC firms, and how those firms can respond to the challenges that lie ahead.

Relationship to text

◆◆ Chapter 11, pages 394–403, "The European Community"

◆◆ Chapter 14, page 530, "Government Role in Exporting"

After studying the text, reading the article, and answering the questions, you should be able to:

◆◆ Identify the EC's current position on the implementation of its Single Internal Market legislation.

◆◆ Discuss the relationship between Community law and national law.

◆◆ Describe the recommendations of the Sutherland Report on the implementation of the Single Market.

◆◆ Explain how product safety legislation negatively affects U.S. firms.

◆◆ Identify measures that U.S. firms can take to counteract perceived discrimination.

Preview

◆ Although 95 percent of the Single Internal Market legislation has been adopted, not all member countries have adopted each piece of legislation.

◆ Communication gaps between the agency responsible for enforcing EC directives and customs officials have caused problems for U.S. exporters.

◆ The Sutherland report identifies a number of recommendations for ensuring that member countries implement EC directives in an equivalent way.

◆ Member states may determine penalties for infractions, but those sanctions may vary.

◆ The EC is closely monitoring the implementation of the 1992 program to ensure consistency among the ministries in each member state.

A Top Priority for the EC in 1993:

Implementing the Single Internal Market

The European Community spent eight years focusing on the legislative aspect of the Single Internal Market program. Now that 95 percent of the program has been adopted, EC member states must turn their attention to ensuring that all these rules are implemented and enforced in a uniform way in spite of differences in legal tradition, regulatory approach, and market circumstances.

U.S. exporters might wonder how effective the enforcement of the Single Internal Market will be despite this optimistic start. There are concerns about how differing national requirements will be harmonized in cases where a member state has not implemented a directive; about the possibility of national laws conflicting with or adding additional requirements to EC directives; and, about the possibility of member states giving different interpretations to a directive. Also, fines and penalties will differ in EC countries since member state legal systems are not harmonized.

U.S. embassies in the EC have not received any complaints from American exporters about problems bringing goods into the EC or moving them around the Community since the Single Internal Market opened on Jan.1. U.S. commercial officers state

that the Community has shown mostly a "permissive" approach in letting goods circulate except where a law has been violated. Still, U.S. exporters should be familiar with enforcement issues and procedures that might affect them. If a company finds that a member state is not enforcing a directive, it can complain to the EC Commission and eventually take its case to the European Court of Justice or to a member state court. However, this process

could be time-consuming and expensive. There are other options that may be quicker and less costly for U.S. companies to take to solve problems with member state enforcement of directives.

Implementation Issues

The Community reported in early February that it had adopted 261 of 282 single market

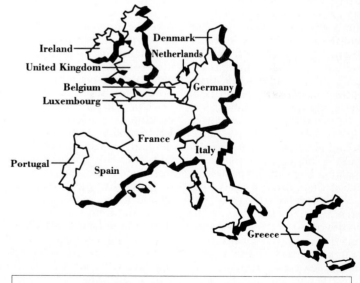

Population & Gross Domestic Product					
1991	Population millions	GDP current - $bn	Per Capita dollars	Exports as % of GDP	Imports as % of GDP
United States	252.7	5,677.5	22,467	7.5	8.8
EC-12	346.3	6,251.7	18,053	21.9	23.4

Source: OECD, Main Economic Indicators, November 1992

directives and regulations. An EC regulation becomes a national regulation as soon as it is adopted. A directive, however, must be transposed into national law by the member states. Directives usually take effect about 1 1/2 to 2 years after adoption to give member states time to implement the directive.

While the EC has pushed member states to implement these directives on time, many directives are in force but have not been implemented by member states. Only 95 single market directives have been implemented by all 12 EC member states. However, 257 measures are in force and 213 directives require national implementing measures. In short, implementation is spotty. For example, while all 12 member states have implemented the directives on pressure vessels, toy safety, and food additives, implementation is still in progress on the computer software directive and the second banking directive even though the EC implementation deadline has passed. Does this mean that U.S. firms cannot derive the benefits of those directives in member states which have not implemented them? The answer is "no," according to EC Commission officials. Community law supersedes national law and companies can act as though the directive has been implemented even if a member state hasn't passed the appropriate laws. Member states have distributed circulars to customs officials to inform them of EC directives which are in effect but which have not been implemented into national law.

In some cases, U.S. firms have adhered to EC directives but their sales efforts have been complicated by national laws. One American university with a branch in Spain was ready to import from the United States 50 personal computers consisting of a keyboard, printer, and computer screen. The U.S. company complied with the EC low-voltage directive. However, Spanish law requires that a Spanish letter ñ be carried on the keyboard. The American keyboards did not have this letter. The U.S. and Foreign Commercial Service (US&FCS) took the case to Spanish authorities. Subsequently, the U.S. exporter was able to sell all the components of the information systems except for the keyboards. The EC has told the Spanish government that requiring the Spanish letter constitutes a trade barrier and must be discontinued. Spain agreed to the EC's order but said it needed time to make the adjustment.

Ongoing member state discussion of a directive could lead to a new interpretation and change the scope of product coverage throughout the EC. This development could affect U.S. exporters. For example, the electromagnetic compatibility (EMC) directive, currently an option for approval, requires machinery to carry a CE mark indicating the product has met EC legal requirements. At this time, the EMC directive does not cover add-in circuit boards for electronic and electrical equipment.

However, on Feb. 4, the United Kingdom Department of Trade and Industry decided that these add-in boards, which plug into existing equipment, should meet requirements of the EMC directive when used in the host equipment. The add-in circuit boards would have to bear a CE mark. The add-in product is not usually manufactured by the same company that produces the host equipment. The U.K. will present this interpretation of the EMC directive to the EC Commission later this spring. In the future, if all member states agree with this interpretation, add-in products will need the CE mark to conform with the EMC directive.

A lack of communication between the national administrative agency responsible for enforcing a directive and customs officials has also led to problems for U.S. exporters. The toy-safety directive, one of the early EC directives, went into effect in 1990. U.S. toy companies met the safety requirements in the directives, enabling them to sell their products throughout the EC. However, when these companies tried to enter their product into Italy, they were told their technical files had to use very particular language in the declaration of conformity—requirements not stated in the directive. These companies were forced to pay an extra expense and take up to two weeks to comply with these national rules. These companies contacted Commerce Department officials who approached the Italian government about this violation of the toy-safety directive. Italian customs officials said they simply did not know about the new directive. The situation was resolved.

The Commission plans to release a guidebook on new approach directives this spring to clear up questions such as what languages technical files should be in.

The EC Commission reviewed in December 1992 the Sutherland Report addressing the issue of implementing the single market. The report, named after the former EC Commissioner, made a number of recommendations for ensuring that member states implement EC directives in an equivalent way so that businesses and consumers would benefit from the single market. These recommendations included: establishing administrative partnerships between the commission and member states; having each member state set up a contact point to take care of implementation problems; forming a committee within the EC Commission responsible for overseeing implementation of the Single Market program; making the sanctions of member state laws for a directive more transparent; having an ombudsman appointed by each member state to settle disputes; and eventually, creating a new European public service to enforce implementation according to EC law.

The Community has just adopted a regulation on product safety that could affect U.S. exporters depending on how it is enforced. The regulation is temporary (two years) and enables customs officers who suspect a product does not meet general product safety standards in the EC to detain that product at the border and notify national authorities. Until some countries like France develop an internal enforcement system, they are being allowed to use customs guards. Under this regulation, national authorities have up to 48 hours to inspect the product and determine whether it complies with EC standards. At the end of 48 hours, authorities must decide whether or not to allow the product into that country.

These new rules for product safety at the border cover food, pharmaceuticals, and toys. EC Commission officials have stated these changes do not signal any greater changes in EC customs practices and that U.S. exporters have nothing to worry about. Most member states plan to inspect for product safety through a "market surveillance" system where inspectors check the products in stores. This new regulation is designed to provide a product safety check for member states which do not yet have fully developed "market surveillance" systems in place. This new regulation could cause some complications. Member states could reach different decisions on what is a dangerous product.

U.S. exporters should note that EC directives allow member states to determine penalties for infractions.

EC INTERNAL MARKET IMPLEMENTATION

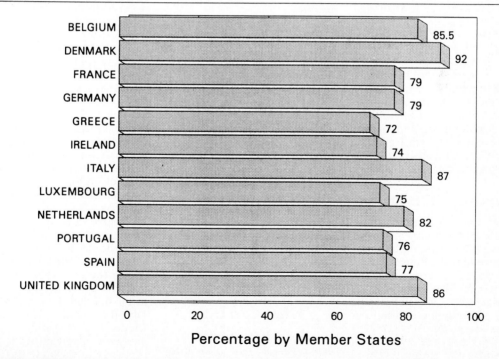

Percentage by Member States

As of Feb. 8, 1993
Source: EC Commission; percent of EC directives in force that have been implemented into national law by EC member states

These sanctions vary among member states. For example, violation of the machine-safety directive is a civil offense in Germany, but a criminal offense in the United Kingdom. The Sutherland Report points out these possible differences could be an obstacle to the single market. The Sutherland Report recommends increased transparency of member state sanctions by notifying the EC Commission.

Packaging and computer software are other areas where member states apply different sanctions to a similar violation. Some member states levy fines on firms violating their packaging laws while the same offense in other member states results in removal of the product from shelves. Computer software piracy is a criminal offense in some member states and a civil offense in others. It has proven more difficult for a U.S. company to persuade a court to order a surprise check for software programming piracy in member states where piracy is a criminal offense, because legal authorities do not view software piracy as that serious.

The EC Commission is collecting data on the fines and penalties member states are assessing for violations to make sure there is not a wide discrepancy. If member states differ significantly in punishment, the Commission fears this could distort trade and undercut the intent at making the single market.

What the EC Is Doing

First, the EC Commission continues to track the implementation of the 1992 program. The Commission records where member states stand on implementation of the directives on its database, Info 92. This database is available to the public by contacting Eurobases in Luxembourg (tel. 011-322-295-0001; fax 011-322-296-0624). Secondly, the Commission is responsible for making sure that member states enforce the single market directives fairly and according to Community law.

Directorate-General 15 of the EC Commission, under the direction of Commissioner Raniero Vanni d'Archiraif, is responsible for overseeing the enforcement and application of the Single Market program. DG-15 has set up two committees to assess problems and to take action if necessary. An advisory committee has established contact points in ministries in each member state charged with enforcing directives under its control—that is, the Ministry of Environment will enforce the environmental directive, the Ministry of Finance will enforce the banking directives, etc. A hearing committee will take complaints on the enforcement of directive from business. So far, DG-15 reports no complaints from business on the enforcement of directives, but admits it is too early to say that enforcement of the Single Market is running smoothly.

The Commission stated that, if an enforcement problem does occur, the members of its advisory committee will contact the appropriate authorities in the member state concerned and try to reach a solution. Ultimately, the Commission can take a member state to the European Court of Justice to decide an enforcement violation. The European Court of Justice has levied large fines against member states for infringement of EC directives. However, the Commission wants to take a low-key approach and contact officials in member states before initiating court cases. Ideally, the Commission wants to act in partnership with the member states to enforce the Single Internal Market program.

What Can U.S. Exporters Do?

If a U.S. firm feels an EC member state is improperly enforcing a directive and the company is losing business as a result, the firm has several options for trying to remedy the situation quickly. First, the U.S. Firm should contact the Department of Commerce's Office of European Community Affairs at (202) 482-5276.

Overseas, the U.S. company can contact the US&FCS officers at the U.S. embassy in the member state in question. US&FCS representatives can contact enforcement officials at the ministry in charge of enforcing that directive and have action taken.

If that approach doesn't work, the U.S. company could contact the U.S. Mission for the European Communities (USEC) in Brussels and ask them to talk to EC officials in DG-15; tel. 011-322-513-4450. USEC officials can talk directly with DG-15 officials to make them aware of infractions affecting the Single Market program.

Over the last two years, the methods mentioned above have worked. The EC does not intend for enforcement differences to disrupt trade with the United States. If these approaches do not work, the U.S. company could take legal action against the member state, which involves a much longer process. The firm could first bring the case to a member state court. These courts can make judgments on community law and the enforcement of directives. The final recourse is for the company to take its case to the European Court of Justice.

Again, indications are that U.S. exporters will not have to obtain a law degree to do business in the European Community; however, they should be aware that the enforcement issue is an important one in the post-1992 European market, that this issue could affect them, and that there are ways to solve the problems that come up. The Commerce Department expects increased opportunities for U.S. exporters in the new European Community market.

Single Internal Market Information Service

- The International Trade Administration has established a central contact point to provide U.S. businesses with information, assistance, and advice on how to do business in the EC's internal market—the Single Internal Market Information Service (SIMIS), operating out of the Office of European Community Affairs.

- SIMIS has been in operation for over three years, working closely with the Department's network of district offices in the United States and with our foreign commercial offices to inform and educate U.S. exporters about commercial and legal changes in the EC market.

- SIMIS staff maintain a comprehensive database of EC directives and regulations, as well as copies of specialized documentation published by the EC Commission, the U.S. government, and the private sector. SIMIS staff track EC technical regulations and standards related to the internal market, and pro-

vide information to exporters on standards and technical requirements, including certification requirements.

- SIMIS offers U.S. exporters a variety of services, including a basic information packet on EC 1992; a quarterly newsletter, Europe Now; specialized guides to EC legislation; information on EC duties, taxes, and customs requirements; informational seminars; and individual business counseling.

- SIMIS staff field business inquiries on EC internal market issues and refer inquires to various Commerce specialists for additional counseling and assistance. SIMIS staff also constitute the core of the U.S. government's interagency efforts on EC standards, testing, and certification and as such the staff answers more than 15,000 out of the more than 70,000 business inquiries per year on standards-related information. Contact SIMIS at (202) 482-5276.

BUSINESS AMERICA (U.S. Department of Commerce): From Bob Straetz, "A Top Priority for the EC in 1993: Implementing the Single Internal Market," *Business America*, March 8, 1993.

QUESTIONS

1. What is the relationship among the number of single market directives identified, those adopted by the EC, and those implemented by all 12 EC member states?

2. When a firm is doing business in an EC member country, should it abide by Community law or individual national laws? What are the problems with each strategy?

3. What is the Sutherland Report, and what are its major recommendations?

4. What is the EC regulation on product safety, and how could it affect U.S. exporters?

5. Use software as an example of how national differences in penalties for infractions of EC directives can affect firms.

6. What is the EC doing to ensure that the 1992 program is implemented properly?

7. If you were a U.S. exporter who feels that an EC directive is being improperly enforced, what should you do?

BEYOND THE EC

The European Community is simultaneously implementing the Single Internal Market and attempting to expand the scope of the EC. These events are occurring in three phases: (1) implementation of the Maastricht Agreement, which will move the EC toward monetary and political union; (2) expansion of the EC to include members of the European Free Trade Association (EFTA); and (3) implementation of Association Agreements with several Central and East European countries. EC expansion will provide challenges and opportunities for U.S. firms doing business in Europe.

Relationship to text

◆◆ Chapter 11, pages 394–403, "The European Community"

◆◆ Chapter 11, pages 406–408, "East European Integration"

After studying the text, reading the article, and answering the questions, you should be able to:

◆◆ Describe the creation of the European Economic Area.

◆◆ Identify EFTA members who've applied for full membership in the EC.

◆◆ Characterize the interaction between the EC and Central and East European countries.

◆◆ Describe the effect of integration on tariffs, standards, government procurement, services, and rules of origin.

Preview

◆ The European Economic Area (EEA) will extend the free movement of goods, capital, services, and people by the EC to the EFTA countries by early 1994.

◆ Bilateral Association Agreements between the EC and several Central and East European countries will reduce tariffs and other barriers, eventually culminating in bilateral free trade.

◆ U.S. firms face new challenges in the area of foreign expectation.

European Integration:

The EC and Beyond

The Jan. 1, 1993, formal date for completion of the European Community (EC) Single Internal Market has come and gone, with great strides having been made toward integrating the economies of the 12 EC member states. The EC member states have begun the process of implementing most aspects of the Single Market program. Simultaneously, the EC is working toward ratification of the Maastricht Treaty on European Union as a vehicle to move toward monetary and political union.

According to many European leaders, this is only the beginning of the process of European integration. Beyond internal efforts among the current 12 EC member states, the EC is steadily building links with its European neighbors. This article will examine some of the areas in which evolving European integration may affect the interests of U.S. exporters.

Current Integration Process

The increase in European integration is occurring within several contexts, among them: (1) creation of the European Economic Area (EEA), (2) countries making application for membership in the EC, and (3) implementation of Association Agreements with several Central and East European countries.

Agreements like the European Economic Area (EEA) will extend the four freedoms of the EC internal market—free to the countries of the European Free Trade Association (EFTA). The timetable for implementation of the EEA has been delayed by the December 1992 Swiss rejection of the EEA treaty. The treaty must be renegotiated and ratified by the other EFTA members and projections now are for full implementation of the treaty sometime in early 1994.

Given such delays in the timetable, it is understandable that several EFTA countries are already looking beyond the EEA to full EC membership. Austria, Sweden, and Finland began accession negotiations with the EC in February 1993 and Norway could join these talks. These applicants have expressed hope that the negotiations will be concluded by the end of 1993, with ratification by all parties in 1994, and full EC membership by 1995.

Looking eastward, trade provisions of the bilateral Association Agreements between the EC and several of its Central and East European neighbors have been in effect since March 1992. These agreements provide schedules for phase down of tariffs and other barriers, to culminate in bilateral free trade areas around the turn of the century. The agreements also set the stage for membership of the associated Central and East European countries in the Community by early in the next century.

All of these agreements will require the non-EC countries involved to harmonize their laws with those of the EC. As this process begins, U.S. firms are becoming increasingly concerned that they will face barriers to exporting in a number of areas, including tariffs, standards, government procurement, services, and origin rules.

Tariffs

By far the most visible issue that has arisen in recent months related to EC integration with its neighbors has involved tariffs, specifically the impact of the EC Association Agreement on U.S. exports to Poland. U.S. exports face increased competition from EC exports which enter Poland at reduced or zero-duty rates under the Association Agreement. For example, since March 1, 1992, a computer manufactured in the United States and exported to Poland is subject to a 20 percent duty, whereas a comparable computer originating in the EC enters Poland duty free.

This has led some exporters to consider establishing manufacturing facilities in Europe, to take advantage of the tariff preferences provided under the Association Agreements. For its part, the U.S. government is working to "level the playing field," by negotiating with the government of Poland to secure duty suspensions in areas of prime interest to U.S. exporters.

The New Europe	GNP/GDP ($Billions)	Population (Millions)
European Community (Total)	**6,267.9**	**346.3**
Belgium	199.8	10.0
Denmark	130.0	5.2
France	1,197.7	57.2
Germany	1,588.0	80.3
Greece	68.6	10.3
Ireland	42.3	3.5
Italy	1,150.0	57.8
Luxembourg	9.0	0.4
Netherlands	270.0	14.9
Portugal	68.8	9.8
Spain	526.2	39.1
United Kingdom	1,017.5	57.8
European Free Trade Association (Total)	**868.55**	**32.82**
Austria*	164.1	7.8
Finland*	130.9	5.0
Iceland	6.5	0.3
Liechtenstein	.65	.029
Norway*	106.9	4.2
Sweden*	230.6	8.6
Switzerland	228.9	6.9
EC Associate Status (Total)	**440.0**	**38.5**
Czech and Slovak Republics	108.9	15.7
Hungary	60.1	10.3
Poland	162.7	38.4
Bulgaria (agreement initialed)	36.4	8.9
Romania	71.9	23.2
Seeking EC Membership (Total)	**206.2**	**60.66**
Turkey	198.0	59.6
Cyprus	5.7	0.7
Malta	2.5	.36
The New Europe (Total)	**7,782.65**	**536.28**

*Have applied for EC membership
Source: Embassies; 1991 figures

Tariffs will become an issue for U.S. exporters into the EFTA countries a bit further into the future: EFTA member countries which join the EC will have to discard their national tariffs and adopt the EC tariff schedules. For some products this will mean a decrease in tariffs, while for others there may be an increase (the EC's average external tariff on manufactured goods is 4 percent, EFTA's average is 2 to 3 percent). The new tariffs will likely be phased in over some period of time, with increases or decreases occurring gradually over a number of years. Exporters will need to be aware of these impending changes and prepare accordingly.

Standards

Over the past several years, U.S. companies exporting to the EC have taken an intense interest in EC standards development and testing and certification procedures as one of the keys to remaining competitive in the changing EC market. EC standards, testing, and certification policies will soon be extended to other parts of Europe, as many EFTA and Central and East European countries begin to fulfill obligations of their agreements with the EC to harmonize their laws and regulations to those of the EC.

The dialogue on standards initiated in 1989 by the Department of Commerce with the EC Commission has increased the transparency of the European standards making process as well as U.S. access to the process. This model should provide a positive foundation upon which to build cooperation on standards issues as EC policies are adopted in EFTA and Central and East Europe.

Current U.S. government efforts focus on establishment of mutual recognition agreements (MRAs) with the EC for testing and certification in key areas of concern to U.S. exporters. The U.S. government intends to seek similar MRAs with the EFTA member countries, in anticipation of completion of the EEA and of membership of these countries in the EC.

In the Central and East European countries, exporters will have to remain aware of country-by-country requirements. Trade-restrictive standards generally have not been a problem for U.S. exports to these countries in the past. However, as these countries harmonize their standards policies and practices to those of the EC, exporters will want to watch for any restrictive use of standards and notify the U.S. government immediately. MRA agreements with these countries could resolve certain problems, for instance where officials from the Central and East European countries decline to recognize U.S. approvals but accept EC member state approvals.

Government Procurement

Bidding procedures for public procurement contracts across Europe will eventually come to be governed by EC-based rules. Under the EEA and the Association Agreements, the EFTA countries and several of the Central and East European countries will move to phase in the EC's procurement regulations, including the EC's utilities directive. Firms in these countries will be able to compete on equal terms with Community firms for public-sector contracts. For U.S. firms this means that discriminatory EC legislation (50 percent EC content; 3 percent price preference) will spread to these countries, making it more difficult for U.S. firms to receive fair treatment on bids for public utilities contracts throughout Europe.

Services

For U.S. exporters, the biggest impact of the EEA is expected to take place in the services sector, since EC-EFTA trade has been duty-free for most industrial goods since the late 1970s. As part of the EEA, the EFTA countries will adopt the EC's Second Banking Directive, which will simplify procedures for European and U.S. banks alike to set up branches throughout Europe. Similar benefits are expected for insurance and securities providers.

The U.S. broadcast industry, however, will likely be worse off as a result of EC integration with its neighbors. The EC's Broadcast Directive requires EC national governments to reserve at least 50 percent of television broadcast time for works of European origin. Most of the EFTA and Central and East European countries currently either do not have or do not enforce quotas on non-European origin television broadcasts. With the EEA, the Association Agreements and the goal of eventual EC membership for these countries, there is a clear threat that these countries will adopt and implement similar discriminatory broadcast quotas.

Environment

EC control over environmental regulation has been limited by elaboration of the principle of "subsidiarity," which calls for EC-level action only when the desired goal cannot be achieved at the member state level. Under the influence of the subsidiarity principle, an enlarged EC could well be marked by increasing divergence between member state environmental rules.

Generally speaking, the northern tier EC member states have stricter environmental regulations, while the southern tier states have more lax environmental regulations. The EFTA member states are also known for their zeal for protection of the environment. If several of the EFTA member countries join the EC by 1995, as is currently expected, then there will likely be an even greater disparity between the environmental requirements from EC member state to member state.

At the other end of the spectrum are the countries of Central and East Europe, which often have very limited rules on environmental protection. If several of these Central and East European countries join the Community soon after the turn of the century, as is foreseen in the Association Agreements, this could yield an even greater divergence in EC member state environmental regulation. Lack of uniformity in environmental regulation and enforcement could increase the costs for U.S. exporters faced with meeting different environmental standards in the larger Europe.

Rules of Origin

The EEA agreement contains preferential rules of origin which will be used to determine whether products are eligible for duty-free treatment within the EEA. U.S. origin products may be eligible for duty-free treatment within the EEA if they have been "sufficiently worked or processed" within an EC or EFTA country. Depending upon the product in question, "sufficiently worked" can mean that at least 60 percent of the value of the product must originate from an EC/EFTA country in order for duty-free status to be conferred. U.S. origin products which do not qualify for duty-free status under the EEA may still circulate within the EEA, but will continue to face duties once at their point of entry into Europe and possibly again when exported from an EFTA country to the EC or vice versa.

Conclusion

The Department of Commerce remains committed to ensuring that U.S. commercial interests are not disadvantaged as the integration of Europe proceeds. Along with other U.S. government agencies, we will continue to take appropriate steps to enhance our export competitiveness throughout the area. We welcome input from *Business America* readers on barriers encountered as a result of European integration.

Please direct any such comments to the Office of European Community Affairs at (202) 482-5276.

BUSINESS AMERICA (U.S. Department of Commerce): From Lori Cooper and Marie Treinen, "European Integration: The EC and Beyond," *Business America*, March 8, 1993.

QUESTIONS

1. What is the European Economic Area (EEA), and what is the timetable for its implementation?

2. Why do you think several EFTA countries are interested in joining the EC, rather than just staying members of the EFTA?

3. Why is the U.S. concerned about tariff-reduction agreements that the EC is entering into with other countries, such as Poland?

4. How will standards development and testing and certification procedures be affected as countries join the EC, and how could those changes affect U.S. exporters?

5. Why will the biggest impact of the EEA for U.S. exporters probably occur in the services sector?

6. What is the principle of "subsidiarity," and what does that mean regarding environmental compliance?

7. How do rules of origin affect the type of operations that U.S. firms establish in Europe?

ARTICLE 11

NAFTA: POTENTIAL BENEFITS AND REMAINING ISSUES

In 1991 the United States, Canada, and Mexico began negotiating a free trade agreement. When operative, the combined market will be the largest in the world. NAFTA will benefit many groups, although not all.

Those interests that anticipate losing ground have allied themselves to either block enactment of the agreement or to gain measures and stipulations.

Relationship to text

◆◆ Chapter 5, pages 169–178, "The Rationale for Governmental Intervention"

◆◆ Chapter 6, page 218, "Rationalized Production"

◆◆ Chapter 11, pages 392–394, "Regional Economic Integration," and pages 423–427, "Case: A North American Free Trade Area"

◆◆ Chapter 14, pages 518–520, "Maquiladora Industry"

After studying the text, reading the article, and answering the questions, you should be able to:

◆◆ Relate the potential positive and negative impacts of NAFTA on U.S. interests.

◆◆ Understand the recent trade relationship between the United States and Mexico, especially the maquiladora program.

◆◆ Recognize the role of special interests in the trade–negotiation process.

Preview

◆ As Mexico's economy contracts or expands, U.S. exports increase or decrease by a greater amount.

◆ Mexico has greatly liberalized its trade since joining GATT in 1986.

◆ U.S. industries with export potential (chemicals, plastics, machinery, and metals) stand to benefit most from free trade, whereas tariff-protected industries may lose the most.

◆ The major remaining issues within the United States for implementing a NAFTA agreement include treatment of dislocated workers, acceptable control over the rules of origin on traded goods, and concern that the agreement will negatively affect environmental protection.

NAFTA:

A Review of the Issues

Because the United States is Mexico's largest trading partner and Mexico is the United States' third largest trading partner, Mexico's economic ups and downs are felt by many U.S. industries. The five largest U.S. exports to Mexico in 1991 were electrical machinery, nonelectrical machinery, transportation equipment, chemicals, and primary metals; totaling slightly less than two-thirds of manufacturing exports to Mexico that year. And the interdependence between the two countries is growing. In 1971, the U.S. provided 61.4 percent of Mexico's imports and received 61.6 percent of its exports. By 1989, those numbers had grown to 70.4 and 70.0, respectively. As illustrated in Figure 1, U.S. exports to Mexico rise and fall with the Mexican economy. During the 1970s, growth in U.S. exports was closely aligned to Mexican gross domestic product (GDP)—that is, changes in Mexican GDP were met by roughly an equal change in U.S. exports. But by the 1980s, the relationship had changed. As Mexico's economy expanded or contracted, U.S. exports increased or decreased by a greater amount. For example, in 1986, Mexican GDP declined 25.4 percent; U.S. exports declined 45.4 percent.

It seems plausible to conclude that U.S. policies that stimulate growth in Mexico could quickly benefit the U.S. One such policy is the proposed free trade agree-

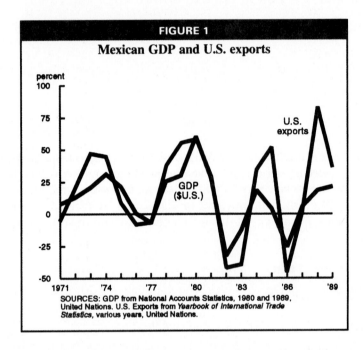

FIGURE 1

Mexican GDP and U.S. exports

SOURCES: GDP from National Accounts Statistics, 1980 and 1989, United Nations. U.S. Exports from *Yearbook of International Trade Statistics*, various years, United Nations.

ment between the United States, Mexico, and Canada known as the North American Free Trade Agreement or NAFTA (see Box 1 for an overview of NAFTA). The potential benefits of a regional trading bloc to these nations are enormous. In 1990, the combined GDP of the three countries was $6.2 trillion, a full $221.3 billion greater than the European Economic Community's. Thus, all three countries would benefit from reduced costs, more competitive prices, and greater global trading power.

This article examines the trade relationship between the U.S. and Mexico[1] over the last few years, and discusses the potential benefits to the U.S. and the Sev-

enth District of NAFTA. It also explores three of the issues negotiators faced during their eighteen months of negotiations that are of particular concern to the Seventh District: U.S. jobs and worker retraining, rules of origin, and the environment (that is, water and air quality).

Trade Initiatives in Mexico

During the early 1970s, Mexico's economic and trade policies were considered protectionist. Foreign investment was restricted and many industries were state owned. Imports consisted primarily of industrial supplies, capital

BOX 1: An Overview of NAFTA
and the Trade Agreement Process

In February 1991, the United States, Mexico, and Canada agreed to begin negotiating a free trade agreement, at the request of Mexico's President Salinas. An agreement among the three countries is expected to benefit all, although at possibly very different levels, and eventually allow each trading partner roughly equal access to the others' markets. Formal negotiations began in June 1991, and on August 12, 1992, it was announced that an agreement had been reached.

Benefits of Free Trade

The direct benefit of free trade derives from the nearly complete elimination of tariffs between free trade partners. It is expected the U.S. will benefit[1] through expanded trade with a large and growing market, increased competitiveness in world markets, and more investment opportunities for U.S. firms. Mexico will benefit from more open and secure access to its largest market, the U.S.; increased confidence on the part of foreign firms to invest in Mexico; a more stable economic environment; and the return of Mexican owned capital. Canada's benefits are mostly in the form of safeguards; maintaining its status in international trade; no loss of its current trade preferences in the U.S. market; and equal access to Mexico's market. While NAFTA will, on net, benefit each nation, it is not a win-win situation for everybody. It produces both winners and losers among industries and occupations; and it must deal with such issues as worker displacement and rules of origin, as well as address issues such as the impact of free trade on the environment (that is, air and water quality).

The U.S. Trade Agreement Process

Under the directive of the Trade Act of 1974, once the U.S. has decided to enter free trade negotiations with a country(s), the President submits a formal request to Congress requesting authority to negotiate with the proposed trade partner(s). Under the act's "fast track" authority, Congress has 60 legislative days to approve or reject the request. During this period, congressional committee hearings are held to solicit comments and testimony from interested parties. If the request to negotiate an agreement is approved, the negotiations can begin but must be completed within 2 years. Once the negotiators prepare a final agreement, it is submitted to Congress for approval and it must be accepted or rejected as is. That is, no amendments or revisions are allowed. If approved by Congress, the President then signs the agreement and the terms and timetables agreed to by the trading partners can be implemented.

The NAFTA Agenda

In agreeing to participate in a free trade agreement, the U.S., Canada, and Mexico developed an agenda of specific trade policies on which the three countries were to agree. The three countries also agreed to address issues and concerns that each country may have about the others' current and future trading policies. Towards that end, working groups were formed to negotiate the following issues:

Market access
   Tariffs and nontariff barriers
   Rules of origin
   Government procurement

Trade rules
   Safeguards
   Subsidies; countervailing and antidumping
      duties
   Health and safety standards

Services

Investment

Intellectual property

Dispute settlement

[1] Benefits to each of the three trading partners are credited to Hutbauer and Schott (1992).

(Continued)

(Box 1 Continued)

Negotiation Results

When the agreement was announced on August 12, the following details, by industry, were provided:

Autos—Mexican tariffs were reduced from 20 to 10 percent immediately on autos and on most auto parts within 5 years; NAFTA completely eliminates auto tariffs in 10 years; eliminates export quotas and performance requirements on foreign owned manufacturing facilities in Mexico; eliminates duties on three-fourths of U.S. parts exports within 5 years; and eliminates Mexican import restrictions on buses and trucks within 5 years. To qualify for duty free trade, autos must contain 62.5 percent North American content.

Textiles and apparel—NAFTA eliminates barriers to trade on over 20 percent of U.S. textile and apparel exports; eliminates barriers on another 65 percent over the next six years; and provides strong rules of origin in order to qualify for duty free status.

Agriculture—one-half of U.S. exports to Mexico will be duty free immediately, with remaining goods to be tariff free within 15 years.

Energy and petrochemicals—NAFTA allows private ownership and operation of electric generating plants for self-generation, cogeneration, and independent power plants; provides immediate access to trade and investment for most petrochemicals; and allows U.S. firms to negotiate directly with Mexican purchasers of natural gas and electricity and to conclude contracts with PEMEX, Mexico's state run petroleum company, or CFE, Mexico's state owned electricity firm.

Electronics and telecommunications—NAFTA eliminates most Mexican tariffs on telecommunications equipment, computers and parts, and electronic components immediately with complete elimination within 5 years.

Financial services—U.S. banks and securities firms will be allowed to establish wholly owned subsidiaries with transitional restrictions to be phased out by January 2000.

Insurance—existing joint ventures will be allowed 100 percent ownership by 1996; new entrants can obtain majority ownership by 1998; and all equity and market share restrictions will be eliminated by 2000.

Investment—Mexico will eliminate export performance requirements and domestic content rules for U.S. firms operating in Mexico.

Land transportation—U.S. trucking firms will be allowed to carry international cargo to the contiguous Mexican states by 1995 with cross border access to all of Mexico by the end of 1999.

Environment—U.S. environmental, health, and safety standards will be maintained, with states and local governments having the ability to increase standards as needed; NAFTA preserves international treaty obligations such as trade limits on protected species and permits more stringent standards to be imposed on new investment.

equipment, industrial and nonauto transportation equipment, and transportation parts. Exports were primarily agricultural and manufactured goods. Manufactured goods were derived largely from the "maquiladora" plants: foreign owned (mainly U.S.) plants that bring unfinished parts and components into Mexico for final processing and assembly prior to reexport into the United States (see Box 2 for an overview of the maquiladora program).

The rise in world oil prices during the 1970s prompted Mexico to develop its huge oil reserves. These reserves, in turn, served as collateral for substantial loans from the rest of the world, and in particular, U.S. banks. Exports of petroleum and petroleum products soared, reaching 75.3 percent of general exports in 1982. But by the early 1980s, world oil prices had topped out, and Mexico could no longer service its debt. New loans to Mexico ceased. Prodded by economic decline, the Mexican government implemented bold economic reforms which stabilized the

BOX 2: An Overview of the Maquiladora Program

The maquiladora program was initiated in 1965 by the Mexican government in response to the cancellation by the United States of a prior work program, called the bracero program, that allowed Mexican workers to cross the border for seasonal work. The maquiladora program allows 100 percent foreign ownership of a firm located in Mexico for the purpose of manufacture and assembly of products for export. In the original program, imports used in processing were not subject to Mexican tariffs providing they were 100 percent reexported. Recent changes to the program allows a portion of the goods to be sold in the domestic market. Only the value added in Mexico (that is, labor costs and domestic parts) are subject to import tariffs upon reentry. Also, machinery or other items used in the production are exempt from Mexican import tariffs.

The textile industry was the first industry to use the maquiladora program but over time, other labor-intensive industries such as electrical components, furniture, and transportation equipment also opened factories in Mexico. Originally, maquiladoras had to be located along the Mexi-

can border, but that restriction is no longer in force. By 1990, 470,000 workers, including both production and administrative workers, were employed in maquiladoras.Most maquiladoras are U.S. owned, but there are a few Canadian, Japanese, and European operations as well. Due to the present state of the U.S. economy, more applications to build maquiladoras were received from non-U.S. companies in 1991 than from U.S. companies.

While NAFTA will eventually remove most tariff and nontariff barriers to trade between the U.S. and Mexico, the fate of the maquiladoras is uncertain. The theory that more U.S. plants will relocate to Mexico to take advantage of lower Mexican wages is not necessarily sound. For one, as the Mexican economy grows, the wage gap will eventually decrease. Also, other factors, such as infrastructure and natural resources, play a large part in location decisions. On the other hand, Mexico is a large and growing market, and the decision to relocate to be closer to a firm's market will become a factor in favor of either relocating or expanding operations.

---

economy, reignited economic development, and opened new horizons for trade and investment. In 1986, Mexico joined the General Agreement on Tariffs and Trade (GATT) and reduced its tariffs from levels of 100 percent, in some cases, to a maximum of 20 percent, which was even lower than the GATT maximum allowable tariff of 50 percent.[2] In addition, Mexico opened up foreign investment in many sectors and privatized many of its former, state-controlled industries. By the end of the 1980s, Mexico realized it would be necessary to solidify its new position as a growing and prosperous economy by integrating itself more closely, in particular through trade, with its two northern neighbors, the U.S. and Canada.

Impact on the Seventh District

Although the benefits of NAFTA to the U.S. at the regional level are difficult to determine, the Seventh District, which encompasses most of the states of Illinois, Indiana, Michigan, and Wisconsin and all of Iowa, should realize benefits through increased exports to Mexico.

Of particular significance to the U.S. and the Seventh District has been the growth of U.S. manufacturing exports to Mexico. As a region, the five District states increased their manufacturing exports to Mexico 90 percent over the 1987–1991 period; U.S. manufacturing exports increased 130 percent over the

same period. Also, roughly half of all manufacturing exports to Mexico over this period were in machinery and transportation equipment, two capital goods producing industries that form the cornerstone of the U.S. and, in particular, the Midwest economies (see Box 3 for recent trends in manufacturing exports to Mexico for the District).

In 1991, exports to Mexico of these two capital goods comprised 68 percent of Seventh District manufacturing exports and 53 percent of U.S. manufacturing exports. The importance of these goods to a growing economy is significant. In order to grow, a developing country needs to build factories, housing, and schools. To support this growth, there must be an infrastructure

BOX 3: Seventh District
Manufacturing Exports to Mexico

Over the 1987–1991 period, total export shipments from District states grew from $35.5 billion to $52.9 billion. Exports to Mexico grew by $1.5 billion over this period, or from 4.8 percent of total manufacturing exports to 6.2 percent.

The five largest industries by shipment value to Mexico from District states in 1991 were transportation, machinery except electrical, electrical machinery, primary metals, and fabricated metals. These five industries increased exports to Mexico by $848 million over the period, comprising 55 percent of total manufacturing export growth.

District exports to Mexico grew in other indus-

tries as well. For example, in 1987, exports of textiles and apparel to Mexico comprised only 1.7 percent of total textiles and apparel exports. By 1991, exports to Mexico had grown 18.3 percent of total textiles and apparel exports. Likewise, wood and furniture exports grew from 1.3 percent to 6.1 percent; rubber exports from 3.5 percent to 9.0 percent; fabricated metals from 1.2 percent to 5.7 percent; and primary metals from 6.6 percent to 9.7 percent. Measuring instruments and miscellaneous manufacturing was the only industry that experienced a decline in exports to Mexico over the period.

Recent Trends in District Manufacturing Exports
(Millions of Dollars)

Sector	1987	%of District industrial exports[1]	1991	%of District industrial exports[1]
Food and tobacco	$43.3	3.6	$117.1	6.0
Textiles and apparel	2.1	1.7	44.9	18.3
Wood and furniture	4.0	1.3	51.7	6.1
Publications and printing	18.7	2.6	51.3	4.0
Chemicals	75.7	2.6	147.8	3.3
Petroleum refining	3.5	1.4	2.5	1.7
Rubber	18.9	3.5	110.6	9.0
Leather	0.7	0.7	2.7	1.7
Stone and glass	14.5	3.0	24.5	4.7
Primary metals	50.3	6.6	206.2	9.7
Fabricated metals	25.9	1.2	169.8	5.7
Machinery, except electric	353.0	4.5	933.2	7.9
Electrical machinery	121.4	4.1	273.5	5.4
Transportation	860.8	6.1	1,004.7	6.0
Measuring instruments miscellaneous manufacturing	123.0	9.7	111.1	3.6
Total	$1,715.6	4.8	$3,251.7	6.2

[1] The amounts in this column represent the percent of total District exports of each industry that are exported to Mexico. For example, in 1987, District exports of food and tobacco to Mexico represented 3.6 percent of total District exports of food and tobacco to all foreign countries.

consisting of roads, airports, sewers, etc. For Mexico, imports of machines and transportation equipment[3] have comprised anywhere from 30 to 55 percent of total commodities imports over the last 20 years. It would be safe to assume that this trend is likely to continue, particularly in the short run, with or without NAFTA. As Mexico develops, the demand for goods produced in the Seventh District, namely machinery and transportation equipment, and the benefits to the District, will also grow.

Labor Issues

Among those voicing the strongest reservations about free trade with Mexico are U.S. factory workers, mainly because they fear that U.S. companies, seeking lower labor costs, will transfer factory operations to Mexico where average compensation costs are far less than their U.S. counterparts (see Table 1). While studies have shown that wages are not necessarily the driving factor in location decisions, it must be recognized that they represent a large share of manufacturing costs. For example, wages of production workers, excluding white collar jobs, accounted for 20.5 percent of value added by U.S. manufacturers in 1990.

In addition, U.S. workers' fears are not entirely unfounded. U.S. companies with foreign affiliates in Mexico increased employment from 1977 to 1989 by 146,000 workers (or 39.4 percent) at the same time that employment in foreign operations of U.S. companies worldwide declined by 8 percent (see Table 2). In particular, employment has grown rapidly in electronics industries and in transportation with each of the Big 3 automakers having auto or truck assembly operations in Mexico.

These two industries accounted for 47 percent of employment of U.S. operations in Mexico in 1989.

While these figures document the job flight to Mexico, it is important to note that other forces are also dislocating American workers, including the movement of production to other low wage countries, such as Taiwan and Singapore, by both domestic and foreign companies. Thus, U.S. jobs lost to Mexico might instead have been moved to another low wage country rather than remaining in the U.S. In fact, some business and labor representatives believe that open borders with Mexico have, so far, helped preserve jobs in the U.S. that would have otherwise been lost overseas. It is argued that, in some instances, access to low wage labor in Mexico has sustained the U.S. share of such production in the face of foreign competition, and may be the advantage U.S. companies need to remain price competitive in world markets. Some supporters of NAFTA[4] even argue that protecting jobs in industries in which the U.S. does not hold a comparative advantage makes both the U.S. and Mexico less prosperous. U.S. jobs "saved" in one industry are merely jobs lost in other industries.

From a U.S. perspective, Mexico's growing economy, together with NAFTA, may have a positive effect on the U.S. economy. A recent Commerce Department report indicates that in 1990, exports to Mexico supported 538,000 domestic jobs and that for every 10 jobs directly supported (for example, manufacturing jobs), another 19 more jobs (such as supplier jobs) are indirectly supported.[5] Also, most studies of the impact of NAFTA on U.S. industries agree that industries with increased export

potential will be winners (including chemicals, plastics, machinery, and metals) and other industries, especially those that have been tariff protected (such as citrus crops, sugar, apparel, and furniture) will be losers. However, on net, the U.S. will likely realize only small or negligible increases in production.

Worker Retraining and Other Assistance

Although NAFTA will be phased in slowly over many years, it is likely to accelerate the labor market upheaval that certain industries and local areas have already experienced. Particular regions, including the Midwest, are highly concentrated in industries, such as the domestic auto industry, that have and are undergoing deep disruptions.

Officially the Big 3 automakers support "a well crafted NAFTA" and expect that increased trade with Mexico "could result in expanded export opportunities for U.S. vehicle and parts manufacturers."[6] Underlying this statement is the expectation that the potential of the Mexican market is so large that American operations will expand significantly to accommodate it.

Even so, U.S. labor lobbied hard to have worker displacement addressed and job retraining included in NAFTA negotiations. While the Bush administration does recognize that job replacement is likely to occur and recognizes the need for job retraining, no formal program was included in the proposed NAFTA. However, shortly after the NAFTA agreement was completed, President Bush proposed a five year, $3 billion per year job training initiative, of which $2 billion per year would be earmarked for dislocated workers.

TABLE 1

Hourly Manufacturing Costs for Production Workers

	1985	1986	1987	1988	1989	1990	1991
			(U.S. dollar costs)				
U.S.	$13.01	$13.25	$13.52	$13.91	$14.31	$14.88	$15.45
Canada	$10.80	$11.00	$11.94	$13.51	$14.81	$16.02	$17.31
Mexico	$1.60	$1.10	$1.06	$1.32	$1.59	$1.80	$2.17

	1985–1988	1989	1990	1991
	(Annual % change in U.S. dollar costs)			
U.S.	2.3	2.9	4.0	3.8
Canada	7.7	9.6	8.2	8.1
Mexico	−6.2	20.5	13.2	20.6

SOURCE: U.S. Dept. of Labor, Bureau of Labor Statistics, International Comparisons of Hourly Compensation Costs for Production Workers in Manufacturing, 1991—Report 825.

TABLE 2

Employment of U.S. Non-Bank Foreign Affiliates

Year	Mexico	Canada	All Countries	Non-Mexico	Asia/Pacific
		(Thousands of workers)			
1977	370.1	1,064.5	7,196.7	6,826.6	1,208.3
1982	470.3	913.8	6,640.2	6,169.9	1,159.7
1983	442.9	900.6	6,383.1	5,940.2	1,170.0
1984	430.0	897.9	6,417.5	5,987.5	1,182.0
1985	465.9	900.6	6,419.3	5,953.4	1,155.5
1986	441.9	905.1	6,250.2	5,808.3	1,210.8
1987	438.1	907.8	6,296.6	5,858.5	1,214.7
1988	460.1	965.5	6,403.5	5,943.4	1,283.9
1989	515.8	945.4	6,621.4	6,105.6	1,416.2
Change 1977–89	145.7	−119.1	−575.3	−721.0	207.9
% change 1977–89	39.4	−11.2	−8.0	−10.6	17.2

SOURCE: Department of Commerce, Bureau of Economic Analysis.

This plan, called the New Century Workforce proposal, would replace the current Economic Dislocation and Worker Adjustment Assistance program, as well as the Trade Adjustment Assistance Act, and would require congressional approval.

Rules of Origin

"Rules of origin" is a trade term which defines the minimum percentage of a country's exported product that must be produced or substantially transformed within the border of the exporting country (also known as "local content"). The term "substantially transformed" means that products that use foreign inputs must go through considerable change (for example, a raw material being processed into a finished good) in order to be used in an export to a free trade partner. The reason for this rule is to limit a country involved in a free trade agreement from using cheaper, foreign parts in its exports and then using its favorable tariff arrangements to avoid higher import tariffs.

While all industries are concerned with this issue, the domestic auto industry, headquartered in the Seventh District, had proposed that a strong rule of origin apply to the automotive industry. In addition to a lengthy phase-in period designed to protect companies with existing operations in Mexico, the Big 3 automakers had suggested that the rules of origin be more stringent in an agreement with Mexico. In the U.S.-Canada free trade act, auto related rules of origin are applied to each plant, with a current minimum of 50 percent local content required. For the U.S.-Canada-Mexico agreement, the Big 3 had suggested that each company, rather than each plant, be allowed to average the local content requirement, with GM suggesting a 60 percent requirement, and Ford and Chrysler proposing 70 percent.[7] NAFTA proposes a 62.5 percent local content rule for passenger vehicles and 60 percent for other vehicles and auto parts based on net cost (total cost less royalties, sales promotion, and packing and shipping).

Environmental Issues

A third issue addressed by NAFTA was the environmental impact of increased production. Environmental concerns usually were voiced by three interest groups: environmentalists, industry sectors concerned about losing their jobs to low cost Mexican labor, and industry sectors that stand to gain from increased trade with Mexico.

Environmentalists fear that increased trade with Mexico will expand already problematic environmental conditions, such as air and water pollution, and increase health and safety concerns for workers caused by lax (or nonexistent) enforcement of health and safety standards. These concerns are not only for the Mexican workers, but also for the spillover effects in many U.S. cities along the U.S.-Mexico border. For example, those concerned by this issue cite the Mexican maquiladora program that brought thousands of Mexican workers and their families to Mexican border towns without adequate infrastructure to house and feed them. This resulted in substandard living conditions in the Mexican towns and in pollution of the ground water and air of both the Mexican towns and the American towns just north of the border.

Industries concerned about losing their jobs to Mexican workers have embraced the environmentalists' cause and are suspicious that U.S. and foreign companies will relocate to Mexico to avoid their own countries' antipollution laws. The environmentalists also fear the U.S. may relax its own laws to remain competitive.

Industries that stand to gain from NAFTA point to the recent progress Mexico has made towards cleaning up its environment. For example, the Mexican government has lowered the lead content of petrol, closed some of its worst factories, and passed new environmental laws modeled after U.S. laws. In addition, one study of the environmental impacts of NAFTA suggests that because of Mexico's abundance of labor, it is likely that the types of industries that will open or relocate to Mexico will be more labor intensive than capital intensive, resulting in less energy use and less hazardous waste.[8]

Environmental concerns prompted the United States to develop an action plan that directed the Environmental Protection Agency to meet with their Mexican counterparts to ensure that comprehensive environmental, safety, and health standards and enforcement measures were included in the agreement. In the Bush administration's 1993 budget proposal, $241 million is requested for border cleanup, nearly double that of fiscal year 1992. However, in a recently submitted environmental plan, no new cleanup funds beyond 1993 have been requested.[9] Other U.S. agencies, like the Food and Drug Administration, the Department of Agriculture, and the Department of Labor, also were directed to participate in the negotiations to ensure that all U.S. environmental concerns were addressed. The proposed NAFTA includes a section on the environment that stresses no reduction in current standards and a move towards harmonization of standards among the three trade partners. This agreement is the first trade agreement to specifically address the environment.

Conclusion

The potential for the U.S., Canada, and Mexico to become the world's largest regional trading block will enhance all three countries' ability to prosper and compete. Mexico will most likely benefit the most from its new standing as a North American trading partner. Its recent moves towards international market liberalization and economic reform have already begun to change the world's view of Mexico in terms of trade and investment; NAFTA will solidify it. The U.S. will benefit not only in terms of increased exports, but also from better and more open relations with Mexico in areas such as drug enforcement and illegal immigration.

However, widespread U.S. support for NAFTA will depend on how well the negotiators were able to protect the wide array of U.S. interests, particularly as they relate to rules of origin, worker retraining and dislocation programs, and the environment. If it is to receive broad based support, the costs and benefits of NAFTA must accrue to those directly affected, rather than unfairly burden or protect the few.

Notes

[1] Because the United States and Canada already have an existing free trade agreement, this article will focus on U.S.-Mexico trade relations.

[2] The likely impact on the United States of a free trade act with Mexico, United States International Trade Commission, pp. 1–2.

[3] Because of the use of different data sources, the term "capital goods" as it relates to exports from the U.S. and imports to Mexico is not totally comparable.

[4] McTeer (1991), p. 6.

[5] Davis (1992), p. 2.

[6] Chrysler, Ford, and General Motors (1991).

[7] Chrysler, Ford, and General Motors (1991).

[8] Grossman and Krueger (1991).

[9] Stokes (1992), p. 507.

References

Davis, Lester A., *U.S. Jobs Supported by Merchandise Exports*, U.S. Department of Commerce, April 1992.

Grossman, Gene M., and Alan B. Krueger, "Environmental impacts of a North American free trade agreement," National Bureau of Economic Research working paper series, No. 3914, November 1991.

Hufbauer, Gary Clyde, and Jeffrey J. Schott, "North Americal free trade: issues and recommendations," Institute for International Trade, March 1992.

McTeer, Robert D., Jr. "Free trade will bring better jobs," *The Southwest Economy*, Federal Reserve Bank of Dallas, September/October 1991.

Position of Chrysler, Ford, and General Motors on the Key Objectives of the North American Free Trade Agreement, paper submitted to the U.S. Trade Representative, Motor Vehicle Manufacturers Association of the U.S., Inc., Sept. 9, 1991

Stokes, Bruce, "On the brink," *National Journal*, February 29, 1992, p. 507.

United States International Trade Commission, *The likely impact on the United States of a free trade act with Mexico*, February 1991.

ECONOMIC PERSPECTIVES (Federal Reserve Publication): From Linda M. Aguilar, "NAFTA: A Review of the Issues," *Economic Perspectives*, 1992

QUESTIONS

1. Evaluate means by which workers in any NAFTA country can and should be protected from hardships of job-dislocation that may result from free trade.

2. What effect will NAFTA have on the maquiladora industry?

3. How do you think global efficiency will be affected by the implementation of the NAFTA agreement?

4. Contrast the scope and impact of NAFTA with that of the European Community.

ARTICLE 12

THE SOVIET UNION IS NOW FIFTEEN NATIONS

The former Soviet Union is now fifteen nations, with overlapping territorial claims among some of the new nations. Ten of the new nations have allied themselves in the Commonwealth of Independent States (CIS); however, Azerbaijan, Georgia, Estonia, Latvia, and Lithuania have not.

This article, which includes statistics for each of the fifteen countries, also examines the economic and political transition problems within Russia, the largest of the new nations.

Relationship to text

◆◆ Chapter 2, pages 47–50, "Democracy, Totalitarianism, and Contemporary Political Systems," and pages 52–56, "The Economic Environment"

◆◆ Chapter 10, the entire chapter, but especially pages 354–362, "Transformation to Market Economies," and pages 364–367, "Legacies of Central Planning"

After studying the text, reading the article, and answering the questions, you should be able to:

◆◆ Understand the difficult transition from political totalitarianism to democracy.

◆◆ Recognize the major issues involved in making an economic transition from centrally planned to market economies.

◆◆ Describe the economic trends in the former Soviet Union since economic and political transition began.

Preview

◆ Although Russians have confidence that democracy will eventually succeed, the lack of developed political institutions forces Boris Yeltsin to create democratic continuity.

◆ Political transition raises questions of whether non-democratic means are necessary to reach democratic ends.

◆ Many troubled geographic areas remain in the former Soviet Union.

◆ GNP, industrial output, and personal income have all fallen during the transition.

Holding Russia's Fate in His Hands:

Boris Yeltsin

The course of true reform never has run smooth in Russia. As President Boris Yeltsin prepares to do battle with hard-line opponents at the Congress of People's Deputies this week, Russians are braced for another bruising power struggle. After seven years of political turbulence, the country is highly sensitized to trouble. Rumors of a coup, a dictatorship, social upheaval have raced through the capital. But something else has happened as well. Most of Russia's 150 million citizens are taking the latest crisis in stride, indifferent to all the fuss in Moscow. However imperfect their experiment in democracy has proved so far, they have gained confidence that one day it will succeed.

At the moment, their faith is pinned on Boris Nikolayevich Yeltsin. He is too much the populist President to take comparisons with King Louis XIV of France very kindly. But anyone who looks at how power is wielded in Russia today cannot help seeing that, to paraphrase the boastful French monarch, *L'etat c'est Yeltsin*. The Russian leader never aspired to the role of Sun President, around whom everything in the realm turns. But he so dominates the political landscape that it would be no exaggeration to say that as Yeltsin goes, so goes the nation.

Under his leadership, Russia has taken major strides toward becoming a free and open society. The disastrous state of the economy he inherited has made it exceptionally difficult, but his reform team is doing much better than many Western analysts expected. Yet it would be foolhardy for the West to turn its back on Russia just because the ideological conflicts of the cold war are over. The burden that Yeltsin must carry is too heavy for one man. If he should falter, the consequences will reverberate around the world. Russia, says Gennadi Burbulis, Yeltsin's chief political strategist, has become "the prism through which a universal longing for global change has been focused."

The trouble is that one year after the collapse of the Soviet Union, Russia still lacks the kind of political institutions that would ensure the continuity of reforms without Yeltsin. Attempts to establish a system of checks and balances are not faring well. The legislature is paralyzed by unending battles with the executive branch. The new constitutional court must work without a proper constitution. The government has to listen to such a deafening chorus of calls for its resignation that ministers cannot concentrate on the business of reform. It falls to the President to keep the operation of state on track. Says Burbulis: "The majority of Russians have confidence not in institutions like the parliament and

government but in the person of the President. During a transformation of such magnitude this kind of personification of power can be positive, but it is also dangerous."

Russia is not the only part of the former Soviet Union to find the transition from totalitarian rule to democracy rocky. The new states have learned that it is not enough to establish a presidential form of rule if there are not local democratic traditions to sustain it. During the past year, new Presidents have been overthrown in the former republics of Georgia, Azerbaijan and Tajikistan. In the Central Asian nation of Turkmenistan, President Saparmurad Niyazov is reviving the tradition of the communist personality cult, complete with marching columns of youths dressed in T shirts emblazoned with his portrait.

So far Yeltsin has proved immune to efforts by sycophantic followers to turn him into an uncrowned Czar. He is a true man of the people—a real muzhik, as the Russians say—who works in his own garden and loves to eat herring with boiled potatoes. To maintain the common touch, he often stops his official motorcade to chat with people on the street. Although he has an unfortunate habit of making promises dictated by the feelings of the moment, he has been courageous in supporting unpopular economic policies that have eroded his standing among ordinary citizens.

Yeltsin has tried out a variety of roles in his quest to be the kind of strong executive he thinks Russia needs. After he was chosen chairman of the supreme soviet in May 1990, he did a stint as parliamentary leader. A year and one month later, he became the first popularly elected President in the country's history. He even took on the second job of Prime Minister for several months in October 1991. None of these has quite fit the bill. The irony is that Yeltsin is haunted by the same problem that plagued his rival, Mikhail Gorbachev, when the former Soviet President was trying to create a new structure of power to replace Communist Party rule: he has more authority on paper than in practice.

The dilemma can be summed up in two questions: Should authoritarian methods be used to advance the cause of democratic reform? When is the use of force justified in defense of law and order? These issues resonate deeply in a nation where totalitarian leaders used to violate basic human rights as a matter of course. Gorbachev never resolved the conflict of how to be a strong President without sliding into totalitarian rule. Yeltsin is still feeling his way. Whenever he begins to talk tough in response to turmoil in the ethnic enclaves of the Russian Federation or the latest challenge from parliament, the opposition immediately warns of a coming dictatorship.

Russia desperately needs a new constitution to codify the nation's guidelines. The project has been caught in a dispute between Yeltsin and the parliament over what kind of state structure to enshrine in the new basic law. Yeltsin wants a strong President, who will have a free hand to organize new government structures and appoint ministers. His whole approach is anathema to legislators who want to give parliament the power to control government appointments and to make the head of state a figurehead that Yeltsin supporters claim would be akin to the British Queen.

Western governments operate successfully on both models. But the particular state of politics in Russia tilts the balance in favor of Yeltsin. Far from being a driving force for change, the current two-tier parliament, made up of a permanently working supreme soviet and a larger Congress of People's Deputies that meets at least twice a year, has turned into a major bastion of communist and conservative opposition to reform. The legislature is a cross section, frozen in time, of political forces active in the Soviet Union back in 1990, when the last elections were held and Communist Party influence remained strong.

As things now stand, Yeltsin is saddled with what he views as an obstreperous bunch of foot draggers until their terms expire in 1995. He could try to use the special powers that the parliament granted him after the abortive coup attempt in August 1991 to disband the legislature altogether and impose direct presidential rule. But many fear such a risky step, and parliamentarians were quick to call Yeltsin's bluff by summoning the People's Deputies into session—over his heated opposition—on Dec. 1, the very day his mandate to rule by decree expires.

Yeltsin may talk tough, but he has left the door open for compromise. The government reached an accord, of sorts, last week with the Civic Union, the opposition group representing the interests of powerful Russian industrialists. Yeltsin agreed to restore some state controls over the economy during the transition to a free market. In another move aimed at defusing political tensions, Deputy Prime Minister Mikhail Poltoranin, an archenemy of the hard-liners, stepped down. He wanted, he said, "to protect the President from mounting attacks from an opposition bent on revenge."

On the eve of the congress, the Yeltsin team also floated a plan for a "constitutional agreement" with parliament. The scheme called for a 12-to-18-month "stabilization" period during which the powers of the President, the parliament and the government would be redefined. Since Yeltsin would undoubtedly have to impose limitations on the parliament to make the plan work, rebellious deputies seem unlikely to buy it, even if the President agrees to shake up his Cabinet in the bargain.

Yeltsin has already tried to outmaneuver the parliament by setting up extragovernmental agencies that are answerable only to the President. Yet even Yeltsin's democratic supporters were concerned when he established a new security council to oversee defense, security, police and foreign-policy issues, with Yuri Skokov, an elusive apparatchik from the military-industrial sector, as chief of staff. It reminds too many people of the party's old secret Politburo. Yeltsin has also set up special commissions that report to him personally to deal with the agricultural crisis and the growing crime rate. Such moves have prompted the conservative daily Pravda to warn that the President was creating "a supreme authority in the country whose decisions cannot be questioned."

The Yeltsin team has been toying with other options to

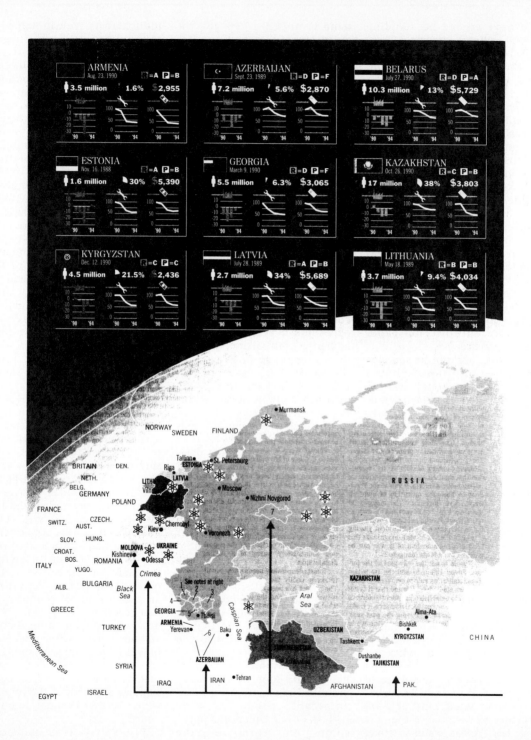

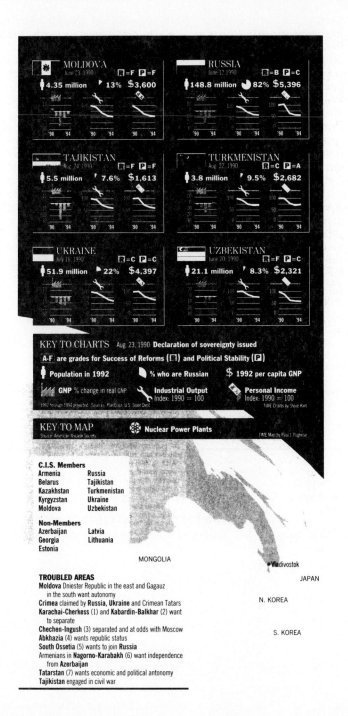

MOLDOVA
June 23, 1990   🅡=F 🅟=F
👤 4.35 million   ▶ 13% $3,600
'90 '94

RUSSIA
June 12, 1990   🅡=B 🅟=C
👤 148.8 million   ● 82% $5,396
'90 '94

TAJIKISTAN
Aug. 24, 1990   🅡=F 🅟=F
👤 5.5 million   ▶ 7.6% $1,613
'90 '94

TURKMENISTAN
Aug. 22, 1990   🅡=C 🅟=A
👤 3.8 million   ▶ 9.5% $2,682
'90 '94

UKRAINE
July 16, 1990   🅡=C 🅟=C
👤 51.9 million   ▶ 22% $4,397
'90 '94

UZBEKISTAN
June 20, 1990   🅡=F 🅟=C
👤 21.1 million   ▶ 8.3% $2,321
'90 '94

KEY TO CHARTS   Aug. 23, 1990: **Declaration of sovereignty issued**

A-F are grades for Success of Reforms (🅡) and Political Stability (🅟)

👤 **Population in 1992**   ● **% who are Russian** $ **1992 per capita GNP**

🏭 **GNP** % change in real GNP   🔧 **Industrial Output** Index: 1990 = 100   ◈ **Personal Income** Index: 1990 = 100

1992 through 1994 projected. Sources: PlanEcon, U.S. State Dept.   TIME Charts by Steve Hart

KEY TO MAP   ❈ **Nuclear Power Plants**
Source: American Nuclear Society   TIME Map by Paul J. Pugliese

C.I.S. Members
Armenia	Russia
Belarus	Tajikistan
Kazakhstan	Turkmenistan
Kyrgyzstan	Ukraine
Moldova	Uzbekistan

Non-Members
Azerbaijan	Latvia
Georgia	Lithuania
Estonia	

MONGOLIA

● Vladivostok

JAPAN

N. KOREA

S. KOREA

TROUBLED AREAS
Moldova Dniester Republic in the east and Gagauz in the south want autonomy
Crimea claimed by **Russia, Ukraine** and Crimean Tatars
Karachai-Cherkess (1) and **Kabardin-Balkhar** (2) want to separate
Chechen-Ingush (3) separated and at odds with Moscow
Abkhazia (4) wants republic status
South Ossetia (5) wants to join **Russia**
Armenians in **Nagorno-Karabakh** (6) want independence from **Azerbaijan**
Tatarstan (7) wants economic and political antonomy
Tajikistan engaged in civil war

break the deadlock between the rival branches of power. One would be to turn directly to the people, as Gorbachev did in March 1991 when he held a national referendum on a new Soviet Union. Radical democratic groups have long been prodding Yeltsin to put the parliament-or-President question to a similar vote. Another referendum topic that some economists believe to be absolutely crucial to the success of Yeltsin's reforms is whether land ought to be bought and sold: without private property laws, capitalism cannot flourish. The President says he is considering putting both questions to a plebiscite by the spring of 1993.

But Russia is not Switzerland, a small country where public referendums have a long tradition.

Such calls to let the people make decisions directly illustrate the troubles that democratic forces have had in moving Russia toward the kind of multiparty system that is at the heart of Western-style representative democracy. The collapse of the Communist Party created a vacuum that none of the multitudinous new movements and parties has been able to fill. Many of the fledgling parties are identified with the personalities that lead them rather than any real programs to meet the needs of Russia's emerging society. Since no elections are scheduled for the near future, they are all in effect lobbying groups, vying for the President's ear.

In many ways, Yeltsin is a master politician, determined to get politics off the national agen-

da so that Russia can finally buckle down to work. Many of his tactical moves appear to be prompted by a desire to hold the forces of reaction in check long enough for a new society to emerge, where economic self-interest will prevail over the political passions of the past. He also seems to be sincere in his intention to devolve power from a small group of players in Moscow out into the vast reaches of the country. But the paradox Yeltsin must ultimately resolve is whether he is willing to use his own political power to the full in order to one day give power back to the people.

TIME: "Holding Russia's Fate in His Hands," December 7, 1992, *Time.* Copyright © 1992 The Time Inc. Magazine Company. Reprinted with permission.

QUESTIONS

1. Within the historically planned economies, is it possible to effect economic transition without political transition, or vice versa?

2. What new political risks are associated with doing business in historically planned economies?

3. Why has the former USSR split into fifteen different states? Why did this division not happen before?

4. Why has the Russian economic performance deteriorated during the period of transition?

A R T I C L E 13

CHANGING PATTERNS OF MULTINATIONALS

The image of multinational enterprises perturbs many constituents in smaller and poorer countries who believe these companies can exert undue influence over them.

Although large firms from industrial countries still dominate global FDI, the accompanying article illustrates that the pattern is changing.

Relationship to text

◆◆ Chapter 1, pages 27–28, "Direct Investor Description: Country of Origin"

◆◆ Chapter 2, pages 73–75, "The Multinational Enterprise"

◆◆ Chapter 6, pages 222–224, "Advantages of Direct Investors"

◆◆ Chapter 12, pages 435–454, "The Impact of the Multinational"

◆◆ Chapter 13, pages 468–471, "Needs and Alternatives for Fulfillment"

After studying the text, reading the article, and answering the questions, you should be able to:

◆◆ Describe MNEs in terms of size and origin.

◆◆ Understand the reasons for the love-hate relationships of host societies with MNEs.

◆◆ Recognize how bargaining power affects the terms by which MNEs operate abroad.

◆◆ Discern changing MNE attributes and their effects on traditional bargaining relationships with host governments.

Preview

◆ Most publicity on MNEs relates to giant firms from industrial countries, especially on their operations in LDCs.

◆ Empirical evidence on the political effects of MNEs tends to counter alarmist concerns.

◆ The number of foreign direct investments by smaller firms and firms from LDCs is increasing.

◆ Opportunities do exist in LDCs for small companies prepared to overcome obstacles.

Producing Prosperity

Multinationals in the Developing World

Economic Cooperation and Development (OECD) has suggested that MNC investments have generally contributed to increased per-capita incomes and higher standards of living. While economic development does not necessarily require FDI, as the cases of South Korea and Japan clearly demonstrate, countries that have encouraged MNC involvement—such as Singapore, Hong Kong, Thailand and Malaysia—have experienced economic growth rates well above average. Perhaps recognizing this fact, the developing countries themselves have displayed a cautious but marked interest in attracting MNC investments in the last decade.

It is ironic, however, that the developing world's wary interest in FDI emerges at a time when the worldwide demand for foreign capital is particularly high and the supply is especially low. Speculation abounds as to whether LDCs will be able to attract foreign investment away from the booming newly industrialized countries (NICs) in the Pacific Rim and capital-starved Eastern Europe, especially at a time when commercial lending sources, fearful of reliving the debt crises of the 1970s and 1980s, remain extremely cautious. As the worldwide recession continues, traditional multinational capital sources, from IBM to General Motors, are regularly posting annual losses, and devel-

oped countries remain mired in a painful period of economic stagnation. For all these reasons, the current global economic climate appears unpropitious for those LDCs hoping to finance industrialization through FDI.

A New Course in Vietnam

Fortunately, LDCs are in a better position to capitalize on FDI than economic theory would predict. The changing nature of multinational involvement in developing countries has mitigated the adverse effects on LDCs of the global economic slow-down and tight-fisted policies of commercial lenders. Vietnam is a case in point. With a per capita GNP of about US $200, Vietnam is one of the poorest countries in the world. The US-led embargo imposed after Vietnam's invasion of Cambodia continues to deter aid and investment from the United States and its allies, as well as from international agencies such as the International Monetary Fund (IMF) and the World Bank. It was in this unfavorable investment climate that the Vietnamese government, despite its ideological opposition to private enterprise, opened the country to foreign capital in 1987.

Traditional analysis would conclude that Vietnam's attempts to attract foreign investment have failed, as few "big-name" MNCs have any significant presence in the country. Yet the

numbers tell a different story: in the first two quarters of 1991 alone, the government approved some 200 projects with foreign firms, a total investment of US $2.1 billion. The MNCs that Vietnam has attracted are relative unknowns, such as the Advance Pacific Corporation, Industrial Marketing Group and Overseas Telecommunications International. Traditional MNC home countries are also conspicuous by their absence or relative insignificance. Of the projects approved in 1991, about a hundred involved MNCs from Taiwan and Hong Kong. In contrast Britain, France and Canada, the most prominent Western nations investing in Vietnam, together secured only 43 projects.

While the US embargo on trade with the country is becoming increasingly porous, it is doubtful whether even the impending removal of the embargo in 1993 will precipitate any dramatic changes in the type of MNCs that will invest in Vietnam. Increased Western involvement will most likely follow the example of Britain's Tootal Group. Quick to take advantage of Hanoi's swing toward market-oriented economics, its executives arrived in Ho Chi Minh City in 1988. Within a year, they had signed up a local partner to produce sewing thread, obtained a 10-year tax-exemption for profits and invested US $1 million in machinery for a plant outside the city. By 1992, the company was producing 300 tons of spun polyester thread a year for Vietnam's growing garment industry—a third of which was for export. Both Tootal's experience in Vietnam and Dooyang's success in Venezuela show that fruitful investment opportunities do exist in LDCs for small, dynamic companies that have modest expectations and a good local partner and are sufficiently prepared to deal with a wide variety of obstacles.

The New Multinationals

There are some very logical reasons for the success of lesser-known, smaller MNCs. First, even the most interventionist of governments will encourage the entrance of such firms; this stands in stark contrast to their attitude toward traditional global giants. A Tootal or a Dooyang simply does not have the capital base or political clout to be a significant threat to the national sovereignty of even the smallest developing country. On the other hand, a country like Vietnam may be somewhat wary of inviting Coca-Cola into large local operations, given its unique political relationship with Coca-Cola's home country. Second, the prevalence of so-called "new forms" of direct investment has further stimulated the activities of the smaller MNCs. The OECD defines these new investments as those involving any particular MNC in a minority equity position, with additional contributions to the project being made by local industry, the government or other MNCs. In contrast, traditional MNC activity establishes completely foreign-controlled subsidiaries in the host country. These new investment strategies are particularly attractive to smaller firms precisely because of their "unbundled" nature. A firm is able to convert its unique talents and firm-specific advantages to physical or intangible capital that can be invested internationally, without having to supply all the other assets traditionally incorporated into a multinational investment package.

By encouraging the activities of smaller MNCs, a developing country is able to enjoy three primary benefits. First, there are far more of these companies than the handful of meganationals that have dominated international business over the past two decades. The proliferation of smaller MNCs might therefore engender significantly increased competition among potential foreign investors and suppliers of technology, enhancing the bargaining strength of host countries. This bargaining power can be translated into effective host country demands for increased local control and a larger share of the profits generated by foreign investment resources. Second, participation via smaller MNCs may also increase competition within the host economies. Smaller-scale investments need not crowd out local investment activity, a common detrimental side-effect of the large, monopolistic operations that are the *sine qua non* of traditional MNC activity. Third, smaller firms may also be more willing to share new technological advances than larger MNCs, either because the weaker world-market positions of smaller firms encourage them to penetrate new markets ahead of their larger competitors or because they are less concerned with the long-term risks of strengthening potential competitors. Since smaller firms often lack the means to independently pursue global strategies in marketing their technological advancements, they share new technological advances more

readily than their larger counterparts. Furthermore, the transferred technology is frequently more applicable to the needs of the LDCs than that provided by the traditional meganationals: often, it may be more labor intensive or better suited to the smaller-scale production requirements of developing countries that do not have large local markets.

With smaller firms, host countries may even be able to shop around for various components of each project. For example, to set up a power plant in Bangladesh, a research unit from a large MNC firm may provide the technology, a small engineering firm may provide the engineering and design skills, a local partner could provide semi-skilled and unskilled labor and a management consulting firm could come into play by providing managerial skills or by training local management. Finally, financing could come from local entrepreneurs, or, in the poorest countries, from an international financial institution such as the Asian Development Bank or the IMF. Such diversification of sources helps reduce costs and minimizes the likelihood of transfer pricing.

Indeed, this is exactly what is happening with Dooyang's venture in Venezuela. The South Korean company retains only a 35% minority share in the project, with 20% of the investments coming from Kaiser Aluminum of the US, 15% from the Venezuelan state-owned enterprise Guyanan Development Corporation and the remaining 30% from another small South Korean firm. In addition, a US consulting firm, Arthur D. Little, has carried out pre-feasibility studies for the company and a US investment bank, Goldman Sachs, is overseeing the financial arrangements. US

Secretary of Labor Robert Reich contends that industries that are able to utilize precisely this sort of massively interconnected activity on an international scale are the ones that will be able to maintain a competitive edge in the globalized economy of the future.

Trading Places?

Though many of these emerging MNCs are based in developed countries, an increasing number are coming from developing nations themselves. These MNCs derive their competitive advantage from small-scale or labor-intensive production processes, which makes them well-suited to invest in other LDCs. Most, but certainly not all, of these firms come from wealthier developing nations and the NICs. Host countries in these transactions are predominantly the poorest developing countries, and investments tend to take the new cooperative forms discussed above. For example, as few as 57 out of 602 manufacturing subsidiaries with equities from parent companies based in other developing nations are wholly-owned ventures. The trend is promising both for low-income recipient countries as well as for those developing countries that have some industries with international potential. Thailand and India are particular success stories in the latter class.

Thailand has been actively investing in Vietnam and Cambodia, and for many years relatively tiny Thai MNCs have led foreign investment activities in Burma. Indian MNCs have been a prominent investor in East Africa and the Middle East. The Bombay-based Tata Group, for example, maintains large engineering, textile and oil-refining operations in the United Arab Emirates, Kuwait, Bahrain and Yemen.

New Priorities in India

It would appear that the rise of both small Western MNCs and multinationals based in LDCs, coupled with the concomitant decline of the Western industrial powerhouses, signals the end of an era for global corporate giants in the developing world. While many formerly preeminent multinationals are indeed struggling, reports of the demise of big business in the international arena are greatly exaggerated. What is changing is the type of investment in which they are involved. Foreign direct investment in India illustrates this well. Until the middle of 1992, when economic reforms by Prime Minister P.V. Narasimha Rao finally went into effect, India was committed to the outdated Favian socialist ideal of an import-substitution-based planned economy with massive government intervention in virtually all critical sectors. Since last year, however, the end of the so-called "licensing raj," which required that every industry be licensed by the government and conform to its import-substitution strategies, has prompted a flood of MNC activity. All the prominent players in the international arena—from Pepsi and Coca-Cola to IBM, General Electric and Texas Instruments—have bought into the idea of India's imminent ascendancy into the select club of NICs.

Whether or not these MNCs realize their hopes, a profound shift in ideology has occurred in India—a country that less than twenty years ago forced Coca-Cola and IBM to leave and regularly branded MNCs as tools of imperialist aggression. The message implicit in India's policy reversal was not lost on MNCs.

General Electric in particular has nine of its thirteen business units active in India. Last year it formed a joint venture with Wipro Corporation, India's second largest computer manufacturer, to make CAT scanners, ultrasound machines and other high-tech medical equipment. It also signed three more deals for plastics, lighting, appliances and power generators with the state owned Bharat Heavy Electrical (BHEL).

The efficacy of the Indian government's reforms is also illustrated by the contrasting experiences of Pepsi and Coca-Cola. Pepsi, after five years of onerous bargaining, entered the Indian market just prior to the reforms, in a joint venture with local industrial giant Voltas. After the reforms, however, Coca-Cola spent just three months getting approval to re-enter the market. Even the troubled IBM has set up a joint venture with Tata Information Services to manufacture the PS/2 line. In India, the traditional big name MNCs appear to be the prominent players.

India's embrace of the large MNCs does not mean that the debate during the last decades over the harmful effects of MNC activity on host countries has been decided in favor of those who defend the intentions and prerogatives of MNCs. India's decision to extend a welcome mat to large firms reflects not so much its "giving in" to MNCs as it does India's realization that MNC activity need not imply MNC control. Previously closed countries such as India, Kenya, Pakistan and even Vietnam and Burma have significant local industries that have been sheltered within closed import-substitution regimes. Though highly inefficient in the past, they are capable of remarkable success if trade barriers are removed and if they receive an infusion of financial capital, technology and managerial and marketing expertise from a MNC.

This is exactly what has happened in India as the door to foreign investment has opened in recent years. Most of the operations started in India within the last year, for example, have been joint ventures with large local firms like Voltas, Wipro and BHEL. In contrast, MNC activity during the 1950s and 1960s, the period to which much of the debate dates back, was focused on setting up wholly-owned subsidiaries with the accrual of monopoly as the prime objective. In recent years, the proliferation of new forms of investment, ranging from minor-equity joint ventures to management contracts, has changed the face of MNC activity, making it more palatable to traditionally interventionist economies like India.

New Hopes, Old Realities

Even with the new convergence of interests between developing countries and MNCs, the road to foreign investment in the developing world still resembles an obstacle course. The successes of companies like Dooyang, GE and Tootal mask the far more numerous failed projects, most of which were marred by the rampant corruption, meddling bureaucracy, low-quality infrastructure and ideological barriers that still exist in some LDCs.

The experience of the British holding company Industrial Marketing Group (IMG) illustrates the problem. The small MNC invested US $250,000 to start up an export-oriented timber-processing business in Thu Duc, a suburb of Ho Chi Minh City. Nine months after the initial investment, its Vietnamese joint venture partner, Nhatico, had still failed to obtain a license for the operation. Relations quickly soured. Nhatico managed to get local officials to block an IMG timber shipment, and IMG was left in a precarious position for the next month-and-a-half while it had 1000 cubic meters of lumber idling in a local shipyard. IMG accused Nhatico of hidden motives, believing the local company had hoped IMG would grow tired of waiting for the license and would withdraw, leaving behind its equipment and buildings. Eventually, IMG terminated its contract with Nhatico and found a new local partner.

A similar incident involved Singapore-based Continental Offshore. Frustrated with conflicts within the local government bureaucracy, Continental threatened to pull out its investments in several small sawmills and garment factories in Vietnam. Fortunately, however, its local partners came through just as the deal was about to fall apart. As Continental's chairman Clive Fairfield put it, "The Vietnamese are trying hard to make our venture work, despite the system."

Though daunting obstacles continue to limit multinational activity in the developing world, there seems to be a new recognition on the part of both companies and host countries that significant mutual benefit is inherent in MNC investment. Rather than attempting to ward off the "multinational invasion," developing nations are becoming more receptive toward selected types of MNC activity. MNCs, both small and large, have also realized that accruing monopoly profits and manipulating economically and politically weak nations are not the only ways to guarantee long-term success from foreign investments. This is evidenced by the increasing importance of new forms of investment, such as minority-owned joint ventures, by established MNCs, as well as by the rise of newer, smaller MNCs, many of which are themselves from developing countries or the Pacific Rim NICs.

New MNCs are entering the global arena every day in increasing numbers, while traditional, larger MNCs are changing the way that they do business in LDCs. If pursued intelligently, these new trends could bring about significant changes in the global business environment, with profound implications for the developing world.

HARVARD INTERNATIONAL REVIEW: Shujaat Islam, "Producing Prosperity: Multinationals in the Developing World," *Harvard International Review*, Vol. XV, No. 3, Spring 1993. Reprinted with permission.

QUESTIONS

1. Why might larger firms be more dominant in global FDI?

2. Why would LDCs fear FDI by large MNEs?

3. Why are smaller firms and firms from LDCs now making more direct investments abroad?

4. Why do many LDCs have a more receptive attitude recently to the influx of FDI?

5. Why might FDI by smaller firms be more compatible with the needs of LDCs?

ARTICLE 14

GERMAN VERSUS U.S. FINANCIAL DISCLOSURES

Many German companies are having a difficult time raising cash because (1) the economic slowdown in Europe has resulted in lower profits and (2) the reconstruction of Eastern Germany requires substantial cash, leaving less available for corporate use. Thus, German companies have been looking to the New York Stock Exchange (NYSE) as a place to raise capital. However, the Securities and Exchange Commission (SEC) requires significantly more disclosure of accounting information (transparency) than German companies have historically provided. Daimler–Benz is the first German company to enter into an agreement with the SEC to be allowed to list on the NYSE.

Relationship to text

◆◆ Chapter 9, pages 314–319, "Equity Securities"

◆◆ Chapter 19, pages 702–709, "Factors Influencing the Development of Accounting Around the World" and "Harmonization of Differences"

After studying the text, reading the article, and answering the questions, you should be able to:

◆◆ Identify what agreements Daimler–Benz had to secure to list its securities in the United States, and why.

◆◆ Understand why Daimler–Benz wants to list its securities outside of Germany.

Preview

◆ A hidden reserve arises because a firm either overstates the value of its liabilities or understates the value of its assets; thus its taxable income and dividends are then lowered.

◆ Because German companies are primarily financed by debt, they tend to have large hidden reserves to strengthen their liquidity position for the banks.

◆ The SEC asked Daimler–Benz to disclose its hidden reserves and show their impact on profits.

Daimler-Benz Discloses Hidden Reserves Of $2.45 Billion, Seeks Big Board Listing

Daimler-Benz AG, Germany's biggest industrial group, said it will declare four billion marks ($2.45 billion) in hidden reserves as an extraordinary profit on its 1992 balance sheet. It is making the disclosure as part of an effort to become the first German company to list its shares on the New York Stock Exchange.

The group, which includes luxury car maker Mercedes-Benz AG, has long sought entry to the U.S. stock market but was blocked by differences with U.S. regulators over accounting procedures. U.S. regulators say German companies generally provide too little transparency in their accounts.

Daimler-Benz officials said they were nearing a compromise with the U.S. Securities and Exchange Commission. The agreement is likely to be completed when Daimler-Benz finance chief Gerhard Liener meets SEC Chairman Richard Breeden in New York Monday and Tuesday. The company expects to be listed before the end of this year.

The company wouldn't elaborate but said the accord with the SEC would include the disclosure of hidden assets. The four-billion-mark figure, officials say, emerged as a result of applying uniform valuation methods throughout the company.

"This is money that we've had in the back room," said a spokeswoman, "but it will be visible now."

German companies are notorious for squirreling away cash that never appears on their balance sheets. This is a main complaint foreign investors have about German corporate accounting procedures.

The money isn't expected to be used by Daimler-Benz for investment. Instead, the spokeswoman said the group will retain it as an "internal cash reserve."

The U.S. stock market listing would come at a time of deepening gloom at the company's Stuttgart headquarters. Daimler-Benz's chairman, Edzard Reuter, told German television yesterday that the group's profit dropped about 25% in 1992, but he didn't say whether this was a net figure. Earlier this month, a company spokesman said the group's net income had dropped to the "area of 1.5 billion marks" in 1992 from

1.9 billion marks in 1991, a 21% decline.

Mr. Reuter also said the company faced the prospect of layoffs in its troubled automotive division. Sales of Mercedes-Benz cars, long the backbone of the company, have plunged in recent months, and the company is rushing to trim costs and introduce models to appeal to a broader range of buyers. Daimler-Benz has refused to comment on a report that its domestic car sales plunged 40% in the first two months of 1993.

Getting its shares listed in New York won't solve the company's problems. But it will open access to a vast new capital market. Daimler-Benz has steadily expanded its presence on global stock markets in recent years. Its shares were listed in Tokyo and London in 1990 and in Vienna and Paris in 1991.

Company officials said its modified 1992 accounts would be presented to the group's supervisory board in coming days, and that shareholders would be asked to approve allocation of the four billion marks to reserves.

Richard Breeden, SEC chairman, confirmed that the agency is in talks with Daimler.

"We have been discussing with the company for some time now the ways to try to bridge the differences in the accounting treatments," Mr. Breeden said.

Assuming the remaining details are worked out, he said he hoped the completed negotiations will provide a model for other foreign companies

seeking to raise capital in the U.S. markets.

Questions

1. What is the size of the hidden reserves disclosed by Daimler–Benz, and where will they appear on the financial statements?

2. What will the hidden reserves be used for?

3. How did these hidden reserves occur?

4. Why would the SEC require Daimler–Benz to disclose the value of the hidden reserves before allowing it to list in the United States?

5. In which countries is Daimler–Benz listing its securities, and why is it doing so?

6. Why would the New York Stock Exchange lobby the SEC to relax its standards to allow Daimler–Benz to list?

7. What impact could this agreement have on other European companies?

ARTICLE 15

EMERGING GLOBAL LABOR FORCE

A major controversy arising in industrial countries is the loss of jobs to developing countries. This problem has been a major concern to both Canada and the United States in the discussions on the North American Free Trade Agreement. This article discusses how jobs are moving quickly from country to country to take advantage of highly skilled, low-cost workers. As plants shut down in the industrial countries, replacement ones are more efficient and capital-intensive, and they use fewer workers.

Relationship to text

◆◆ Chapter 6, pages 216-217, "Changes in Comparative Costs," and pages 217-220, "Resource-Seeking Investments"

◆◆ Chapter 21, pages 781-785, "Labor Market Differences" and "Labor Compensation"

After studying the text, reading the article, and answering the questions, you should be able to:

◆◆ Understand the major forces causing a global labor market.

◆◆ Discuss why jobs are shifting from the industrial countries to the developing world.

◆◆ Show how outsourcing affects employment.

Preview

◆ As jobs are lost in the industrial countries, the number of jobs being created in new factories abroad is also decreasing.

◆ Jobs are shifting from America and Western Europe to Eastern Europe and Asia.

◆ New factories overseas tend to be more efficient than their counterparts in the company's home country.

Emerging Global Labor Force

A fundamental shift is underway in how and where the world's work gets done—with potentially ominous consequences for wealthy, industrialized nations. The key to this change: the emergence of a truly global labor force, talented and capable of accomplishing just about anything, anywhere. Says Larry Irving, an executive of Daniel Industrial who moved from Houston to run a factory that his company bought in eastern Germany: "The average American doesn't realize that there is a truly competitive work force out there that is vying for their jobs. The rest of the world is catching up."

Just what is driving U.S. companies—and some from Europe and Japan—to locate that new plant not in Waltham, Massachusetts, or Tucson, Arizona, but instead in Bangalore, India, where 3M makes tapes, chemicals, and electrical parts, or Guadalajara, Mexico, where Hewlett–Packard assembles computers and designs computer memory boards? It isn't only the search for cheap labor. Corporations also want to establish sophisticated manufacturing and service operations in markets that promise the most growth, often emerging nations. The migration of jobs to new lands isn't a straightforward one–for–one proposition either, one job gained there for every one lost to an industrialized country. New technology and the continuing drive for higher productivity push

companies to build in undeveloped countries plants and offices that require only a fraction of the manpower that used to be needed in factories back home. In part because of this, the statistics on the number of foreign workers employed by multinational companies don't adequately reflect the shift of work abroad.

It is far from clear what form the new world of work will ultimately take. But there's already plenty to be concerned about, and excited by, in the transition taking place.

What happens when the corporate drive for greater efficiency collides with the expansion of the supply of labor available around the globe? Will there be enough jobs to go around? Some experts aren't so sure. Says Percy Barnevik, CEO of ABB Asea Brown Boveri, the $29–billion–a–year Swiss–Swedish builder of transportation and electric generation systems: "It is a fallacy to think that industry will increase employment overall in the Western world, at least in our industry."

Barnevik foresees "a massive move from the Western world. We already have 25,000 employees in former communist countries. They will do the job that was done in Western Europe before." More jobs will shift to Asia, he says. ABB, which employed only 100 workers in Thailand in 1980, has 2,000 there now, and will have more than 7,000 by the end of the century. Put it all together, and Barnevik's forecast borders on the apocalyptic: "Western Europe and American employment will just shrink

and shrink in an orderly way. Like farming at the turn of the century."

A. Gary Shilling, an economist in Springfield, New Jersey, predicts the overhang of workers will hold down wages all over the developed world. "Four years ago people were talking about a shortage of labor" in the U.S., he says. "But with the push for productivity in the West and Japan, and the rise of the newly industrialized countries and Mexico and Indonesia, we will have a surplus." Technology and capital move easily around the world, he observes, and the only things likely to stay put are locally produced services, like haircutting. "Unless you have labor that is uniquely suited to what you're doing, there is no assurance the entire process won't move to another place."

The trend unfolding is likely to be more complex, uneven, and subtle than Shilling and Barnevik paint it. Interviews with executives around the globe reveal that increasingly sophisticated work is indeed being parceled out to far-away nations, whose labor forces are exceedingly capable. Says a top executive at Siemens, the giant German industrial and electronics company: "Thirty years ago they could barely spell 'steam turbine' in India. Now we are building the biggest ones in the world there."

The move toward a global work force takes many forms and consists of far more than a stampede to backward low–wage countries. For example, American direct foreign investment still appears to be creating jobs at factories and operations in high-wage countries, primarily Canada and Europe. In 1990, the latest year for which U.S. Commerce Department data are available, American companies employed 2.8 million people in Western Europe, up 4% from the previous year. That was a bigger jump than the 2% rise, to 1.5 million, in Asian workers they employed, or a similar 2% increase in Latin American employees, to 1.3 million. The explanation, in part, is that up until now most direct foreign investment has been aimed at expanding a company's presence in relatively affluent markets.

When work does move to less developed lands, it's by no means automatic that the shift will bring Western levels of employment and prosperity to new host countries. Martin Anderson, a vice president specializing in global manufacturing for the Gemini Consulting firm in Morristown, New Jersey, notes that new factories abroad, even in low-wage countries, tend to be far more labor efficient than their counterparts in the company's home country. That's one reason why counting noses is not a good guide to the value of goods and services produced offshore. "Some of the most Japanese-looking American plants are going up in Brazil," he observes. Not only is the number of blue-collar workers reduced, says Anderson, but staff and managerial employees are as well. Says David Hewitt, another consultant at Gemini: "If companies reduce one million jobs at home through reengineering their work, they may add 100,000 overseas."

The other reason figures on foreign employment don't fully reflect the dispersal of work abroad: Unlike ten or 15 years ago when companies were more vertically integrated, factories abroad owned by Americans, Europeans, and Japanese are increasingly likely to outsource—to contract for parts and labor from independent local suppliers. Outsourcing requires no bricks-and-mortar investment, nor does it add to the employment tallies of the corporation buying the goods or services. Subramanian Rangan, a doctoral student in political economy at Harvard who has studied the phenomenon, says outsourcing is difficult to measure but already large enough to amount to "new channels of trade." Anderson calculates that at least half the value of goods shipped from American-owned electronics factories abroad was actually added at independently owned plants.

How difficult is it to find so-called sourcers abroad? No trouble at all in some industries. Charles Komar, president of a big clothing company in New York that bears his name, says agents for foreign factories prowl through department stores studying the labels on clothing. "I get calls all the time from people saying they know of a factory in Turkey that can sew the clothes for less than I'm paying now."

Janet Palmer, a professor at New York City's Lehman College specializing in the movement of office work abroad, was called by a consultant from California looking for a cheap place to have text and numbers typed into a computer. She told him of typing mills in the Phillipines that would do it for 50 cents per 10,000 characters—approximately five pages, double spaced. A few days later the man called back and announced he had found an outfit in China charging only 20 cents.

Those foreign sourcers are becoming increasingly capable. An example: For years, Ron Ahlers was an industrial designer for J.C. Penny. His job included designing the control panels on the private-label microwave ovens that Penny bought from Samsung Group in Korea to make them easy to use and consistent across several models. One year a while back, when Samsung engineers came to New York to see Ahler's work, they were embarrassed by how much better his designs were than the ones they created for their own brand-name appliances. Ahlers and his colleagues were astonished when one of them said, "The designer will be punished." The proposal from Korea in the next model year was much better. Penny, in fact, soon began shifting microwave design to Samsung. Eventually the U.S. shut down its entire in-house design office.

Visits to the global labor force in places like Eastern Europe, India, and Jamaica reveal just how ready these folks are to handle complex work, but they also suggest the looming oversupply of workers. Says Anderson of Gemini Consulting: "Sit in any boardroom and it is absolutely clear that those countries are the kinds of places in competition for capital. Smart companies see they have to keep technology and capital fluid, and move them to where they can make best use of the advances countries achieve."

"Look out the window from any tall building here, and what do you see?" asks Larry Irving, a Texan, in his not-so-tall office in Potsdam, a town a few miles south of Berlin in what used to be East Germany. "Smokestacks!" That's good news for Irving's company, Daniel Industries, which makes meters that measure the flow of natural gas through pipelines. The smokestacks exist because most of Eastern Europe relied on coal for heating and electricity, and Irving figures there will soon be rapid construction of new pipelines throughout the region—and a market for his meters. That new market looks all the more attractive in light of a slowdown in the company's business back home.

Daniel Industries debated setting up a factory in West Germany, but the cost of land, labor, and buildings was too high. Instead, early this year the company bought the assets of Messtechnik Babelsberg, a measuring–instrument firm that was formerly part of a huge state–run conglomerate in East Germany. Irving is dazzled by the skills and training of the East German workers he inherited. They underwent years of demanding apprenticeship, much like West German workers, before entering the work force. Though not up to speed on the use of computerized technology in the factory or the final product, they are so well grounded in engineering that they are easily trained. Not least, they cost about half as much as West German workers.

But foreign investment can't repair all the problems of the former East Germany fast enough to avoid painful dislocations. Three years ago the plant Daniel Industries acquired employed 600 workers. Bringing in better technology, Daniel needed only a fraction of them to make the meters it expects to sell next year. So despite their impressive skills, the company kept only 60 of the 600. Their low wages have not eliminated the need for large and continuing capital improvements to stay competitive. The company is installing a million–dollar computerized machining tool that will do the work of many workers. Across eastern Germany the actual unemployment rate is approaching 40%. "If you include workers who were forced into early retirement or who will be unable to get work when current train-

ing programs end, it is that high," says Hermann Wagner, an executive at Treunhandanstalt, the German agency that is privatizing East German factories.

In Hungary, General Electric saw an opportunity to acquire a recognized brand name and existing lines of distribution to west and east European markets when in 1990 it bought Tungsram, a big Budapest light bulb maker. What GE also got in the bargain turned out to be a work force that was one of the best in the world at designing and making advanced lighting fixtures. Hungarian engineers are excellent, says Peter Harper, acting finance director at the Tungsram plant. "Give them a concept and they will go out and develop it." The Budapest plant makes automotive lamps used in cars built in Japan and Europe. A Tungsram factory in Nagykanizsa, Hungary, has become GE's leading center for making advanced compact fluorescent bulbs, with many of the bulbs now going to the United States. Tungsram managers are understandably weak in marketing and financial management, but GE has replicated there the executive training programs it offers in the U.S. "With their analytical background as engineers, they handle it very well," concludes Harper.

But Hungary too is suffering an insufficiency of jobs for skilled workers. The official unemployment rate, less than 1% three years ago, is now at 12% and will probably go higher. Tungsram employed 18,600 workers when it was acquired, but a third have been let go

If you thought your job was immune from globalization because you were in a service business, don't go back to sleep. Recent advances in telecommunications technology and aggressive efforts by out–of–the–way nations to boost their educational systems have put wings on

everything from insurance work to engineering and computer programming.

In Jamaica, 3,500 people work at office parks connected to the U.S. by satellite dishes. There they make airline reservations and process tickets, handle calls to toll–free numbers, and do data entry. More than 25,000 documents a day, including credit card applications, are scanned electronically in the U.S. and copies transmitted to Montego Bay and Kingston for handling.

More sophisticated service work travels even farther. A New Yorker calling Quarterdeck Office Systems, a California–based software company, with a question about how to work a particular program will often detect a brogue on the answerer's voice. Beginning at four in the morning, New York time, before Californians are at work, the calls are routed to Dublin, where Quarterdeck has its second phone–answering operation. At the same place, scores of multilingual workers take calls from all over Europe. That would have been almost impossible a few years ago, until the Irish government spent billions to upgrade the country's phone system. It did so expressly to turn the island into a telecommunications–based service center.

Quarterdeck originally used Ireland as a center for translating instruction manuals and software for use in Europe. It gradually came to realize the Irish schools were turning out impressive numbers of technically trained graduates. Increasingly complex software chores were assigned there, and Irish nationals were sent to California to develop original programs. Quarterdeck eventually leased special high-quality telephone lines to link offices in Dublin and Santa Monica, California. Once that connection was in place, it was a small step and little added cost to use the line to reroute customer calls from the U.S.

All across Ireland are dozens of offices devoted to handling complex service work from the U.S. In the village of Fermoy, in County Cork, 150 Metropolitan Life workers analyze medical insurance claims to determine if they are eligible for reimbursement. This is not grunt work. It demands considerable knowledge of medicine, the American medical system, and the insurance business. Met Life's Irish workers also review new policies sold by salesmen in the U.S. for gaps and errors.

Near Limerick, workers at another U.S. insurance company monitor the movement of money in and out of American corporate clients' employee pension accounts to make sure they comply with American laws. The job is far more complex, insists the office manager—who doesn't want to be identified—than mere medical claims processing.

Why do companies relocate work to Ireland? In part because it is cheaper. Operating costs are about 30% to 35% less than in the U.S., says Frank Verminski, head of the Met Life office. And the Irish Development Authority provides generous tax and other incentives worth about a year's pay for each new job created.

Even more important, there appears to be a strong work ethic intensified by a serious shortage of jobs in Ireland. In a nation with only 1.1 million jobs for a population of 3.5 million, Irish men and women consider themselves very fortunate to get a "permanent and pensionable position." The Met Life job requires 18 weeks of training. What is the annual turnover rate in Ireland? "About 1%," says Verminski. "We've lost three

people in three years." The manager of the insurance office handling pensions says the work was sent to Ireland in part because workers in Hartford goofed off so much that managers gave up trying to improve productivity there. Now, she says, "we think all the time of what other work could be handled here."

Ireland is one of those countries that belie the notion that educating your work force will solve all your economic problems. It sends over a quarter of its 18–year–olds off to college—far more than most European countries. But as in India and the Philippines, there are political, cultural, and unfathomable reasons why some nations simply fail to create or attract a lot of industry. In such places, college grads too often end up twiddling their thumbs. Smart managers recognize the opportunity such underemployed grads represent: a big and growing supply of hypereducated workers they can tap into. Some workers may even be willing, or eager, to relocate for a job. Recently a recruiter for Philips, the Dutch electronics company, marched into Trinity College in Dublin and guaranteed a job in Holland to every computer science graduate of the class.

Don't scoff just because you never heard of the University of Limerick or the Indian Institute of Science in Bangalore. Corporate recruiters have, and they are often impressed. Says Stuart Reeves, senior vice president for Dallas–based EDS, the information technology management company: "If you're hiring college types, there isn't a lot of difference in quality across nations. The difference among college graduates by countries is a lot less than the difference among day laborers and high–schoolers. And there's a lot of pent–up talent out there."

In the mid–Eighties, Texas Instruments started setting up an impressive software programming operation in Bangalore, a city of four million in southern India. "We came because of the amount of talent that was available here," says Richard Gall, managing director of TI in India. "We couldn't hire enough software designers in Europe to meet demand, and India was producing more than it could use." And even though TI had to install its own electrical generators and satellite dishes to operate efficiently, wages are low enough that work still gets done for half what it costs in the U.S.

Since TI's arrival, 30 more companies including Motorola and IBM have set up software programming offices in the area, on a cool plateau west of Madras. The 3M company created a software writing operation in Bangalore several years ago. Based in part on the managerial and technical talent it found, 3M began expanding its manufacturing operations, which are pictured on *Fortune's* cover. Its new plant employs 120 people and makes electrical connectors, chemicals, and pressure–sensitive tapes.

Indian–owned software companies like Infosys, with 350 programmers, have sprung up too and are performing work for General Electric, among others. Are Indian programmers any good? "They are less expensive, but that's not why we went there," says Albert Hoser, president of Siemens's U.S. subsidiary, whose parent company uses them. "They do some of the best work in the world."

The potential for a further shift of programming to offshore sites is considerable. Software programming accounts for a third or more of the R&D budgets at many high–tech companies. Says Gall: "As designs and software get more complex, the cost advantage of India becomes greater. We've only scratched the surface of what could happen here."

In the face of what some see as a worldwide glut of skilled workers, a few nations actually experience a shortage of labor. But their drive to boost their own prosperity, by keeping good jobs at home and shipping lower–wage work to neighbors, has the effect of expanding the world labor supply. Japan, for example, uses neighboring countries as a place to offload messy and unpleasant work, such as painting and building construction, that it can afford to disdain.

Singapore is helping to make Asian labor markets more accessible to Western companies. That small country (pop.: 2.7 million) has done such a good job of attracting foreign investment that it began running out of semiskilled workers. AT&T decided to make telephones there in 1985. "The operation was successful beyond our wildest dreams," says Jeff Inselmann, vice president for AT&T's manufacturing in Singapore. Hundreds of other companies similarly set up plants in Singapore. The result: Managerial and technical skills flowed rapidly to the city–state, hastened by special tax breaks to companies that establish regional headquarters there.

But foreigners wouldn't keep expanding operations and assigning more complex and high–wage work to Singapore if the place ran out of factory workers. So the government recently persuaded Indonesia to turn a chain of that nation's islands 12 miles across the Strait of Malacca from Singapore into industrial parks. With a population of 181 million underemployed people crammed mostly on the island of Java, Indonesia was happy to cooperate. In less than two years, more than 40 compa-

nies, including AT&T, Thomson, and Sumitomo Electric Industries, have established factories in the new parks, chiefly on Batam Island, two–thirds the size of Singapore.

Batam is still mostly raw jungle, criss–crossed by roads carved out of the bright red earth and dotted with factories, dormitories, and radio towers. Labor shortage: AT&T set up its factories and recruited 700 workers from Java and Sumatra in eight months. Their pay is a third the cost of comparable labor in Singapore. Batam's population is expected to grow sixfold, to 700,000 by the end of the decade.

Which leaves Singapore free to do what it does very well: design and manage, often for American and European corporations, and help them make efficient use of local labor and talent. Hewlett–Packard's new portable inkjet printer business is run from Singapore—design, manufacture, and profit responsibility. Singaporeans designed and manufacture two popular pagers for Motorola—one accepts voice message, the other is the size of a credit card. Originally meant for Asian markets, they have proved so popular that Motorola is beginning to ship them to the U.S.

Though the bulk of Motorola's research is still done in the U.S., the company is expanding the amount of R&D work performed in Southeast Asia. AT&T Bell Laboratories already has researchers there. Should American engineers be panicked that their jobs could go abroad? Says William Terry, executive vice president at Hewlett–Packard: "Panicked? No. America will always be an attractive market. People will want to buy things designed and made in the U.S. But worried? Yes."

What happens when these deep, heretofore inaccessible pools of labor and talent are plumbed by the rest of the indus-

trialized world? That will depend in part on the pace of change. Will wealthy nations and companies have the time and the wits to adapt their skills and organizations to take advantage of the change, perhaps moving on to some new, higher form of economic activity? Will prosperity come fast enough to countries long denied it that workers won't riot in a revolution of rising expectations?

It's clear that there is something almost incomprehensibly vast going on—a realignment perhaps, as Percy Barnevik suggests, on the order of the end of the agricultural era in Western nations, when people moved off the land and into cities for factory work. Says Gemini's Anderson: "It's some sort of shift from the industrial age to an information age. But it's not that simple. People will still need cars and refrigerators, and people will have to make them. I'm not sure I know exactly what it is."

In the face of such change, whatever form it eventually takes, one should keep in mind a few emerging verities: More than ever before, work will flow to the places best equipped to perform it most economically and efficiently. For one thing, the speed and thoroughness of information delivery in the Nineties guarantee that managers will now know where work can best be done.

To try to restrict the flow of work in the name of saving jobs in this country or that is futile, certainly in the long run. Some nations may succeed at it for a short time, but the cost will be punishing dislocations. It would, for example, be ridiculous and dangerous for the U.S. to try to "staunch the flow of jobs to Mexico," as protectionists might describe it. True, open trade with Mexico will mean that some jobs in the U.S. may disappear, but they wouldn't have lasted long anyway, given the pressures of foreign competition. And with U.S. exports likely to go up substantially, many more jobs will be created—on both sides of the border.

As in the past, countries will do well economically if they concentrate on doing what they do best, pursuing policies that will enhance those industries and services in which they can add the most value. Their particular com-

petence may change over time; consider the example of Singapore. But the prize will consistently go to those countries eager to embrace the new.

QUESTIONS

1. Does the number of foreign workers employed by multinational companies adequately reflect the shift of work abroad? Explain.

2. What factors are causing a surplus of labor?

What might that impact be on labor in industrial countries?

3. Why are foreign investors moving to outsourcing versus vertical integration?

ARTICLE 16

CIVIL RIGHTS ACT OF 1991

The U.S. Supreme Court ruled in 1991 that U.S. laws barring discrimination do not apply to the operations of U.S. firms abroad. However, shortly thereafter, a new law was enacted that extends the jurisdiction of antidiscrimination laws to foreign operations as well. Its provisions and major implications are outlined in the following article.

Although the article focuses on female expatriates, the law is also applicable to race, national origin, and religion.

Relationship to text

◆◆ Chapter 3, pages 91–93, "Group Affiliations"

◆◆ Chapter 21, pages 769–770, "Reasons for Using Expatriates," and pages 771–772, "Local Acceptance"

After studying the text, reading the article, and answering the questions, you should be able to:

◆◆ Describe how access to international posts is related to career advancement into upper-level management positions.

◆◆ Understand the extent to which women and minorities have been employed in expatriate posts within U.S. multinational firms.

◆◆ Outline means to facilitate the movement of minorities into foreign assignments.

Preview

◆ U.S. managers have become more reluctant to accept foreign posts; however, female managers see foreign assignments as a requisite for advancement into upper-level positions.

◆ Women maintain a small percentage of foreign posts, although the percentage has been increasing.

◆ A potential dilemma may result if, by custom, a class of employees is excluded from certain jobs.

American Female Expatriates and the Civil Rights Act of 1991:

Balancing Legal and Business Interests

American multinational companies are facing a growing list of conflicting realities as they staff their international divisions. Primary among them is that managers currently based in the United States are reluctant to accept transfers to foreign posts. Meanwhile, an increasing number of managers in any organization are women, many anxious to attain greater status in the firm and interested in accepting positions that will offer visibility and challenge. This interest is legally protected under the provisions of the Civil Rights Act of 1991.

At the same time, companies with operations in many parts of the world must still deal with local mores, customs, and laws. And those local traditions and preferences often differ from—if they are not in total contrast to—American practices. Reconciling these facts while meeting staffing needs adds to the challenges faced by globally oriented companies.

Staffing Foreign Posts

Filling foreign operation positions has long been difficult for many American companies. Upwardly mobile managers have feared that if they were no longer near corporate headquarters for an extended period they would be forgotten. This has been especially true in firms where senior management had historically downplayed the importance of international experience.

There may now be an impetus to reverse this attitude, because the level of vulnerability American firms face from global competitors is changing rapidly. In 1984, 70 percent of firms in U.S. domestic markets faced significant foreign competition; by 1987, the figure was estimated to be 80 percent. As more companies begin to expand their global presence or meet the international challenge domestically, they are finding that a more positive stance may be necessary to encourage the best managerial candidates.

Some U.S. corporations are already beginning to imitate European, Japanese, and Australian firms, which refuse to send any manager on an international assignment unless that person is identified as possessing senior management potential. At Du Pont, for example, almost half of the company's sales are foreign sales. This is making a stint overseas almost essential for promotion to top management.

Women in Management

Women currently account for approximately 41 percent of the managers in the U.S. work force; however, they account for only 6.6 percent of corporate executives. As companies begin to value international experience as necessary for executive positions within a firm, it becomes more expedient for women to participate in those assignments.

Historically, women were discouraged from applying for foreign postings. The differing attitudes of world cultures toward the "male" and "female" role was generally given as the rationale. In addition, there was no legal requirement placed on U.S. companies to consider women for such positions.

Although women still hold a very small percentage of expatriate managerial positions, there has been a marked increase in recent years. A study of American women sent overseas (Taylor et al. 1975) found that a typical assignment lasted less than 30 days. Only one woman of the 291 women transferred overseas by 171 American multinational companies had been assigned to an expatriate position for longer than six months.

Nancy Adler's multi-part study (1984) of expatriate managers showed that of the 13,338 expatriates from 686 U.S. and Canadian firms responding, 402 (3 percent) were female. Adler defined an expatriate as an employee who has been assigned to a professional or managerial position in a country outside the home base of the company for six months or longer.

By 1989, women's representation had risen to 5 percent of American employees on overseas assignments. In a more recent study, J. Stewart Black (1991) found that 6 percent of the 174 respondents who had spent 9 months or more on foreign assignment were female. However, during the same time period, only 1.3 percent of expatriates in the Asian sectors of the Pacific rim were women (Stone 1991). These figures demonstrate increased female participation on longer overseas assignments but do not indicate that their distribution is equal throughout the globe.

Civil Rights Act of 1991

With the passage of the Civil Rights Act of 1964, women and legally defined minorities were granted certain workplace protections. Title VII of the act prohibits discrimination in employment based on gender, race, national origin, or religion. However, until the passage of the Civil Rights Act of 1991, Title VII protections were not relevant to American citizens working abroad for U.S.-controlled firms. A long-standing principle of American law is that Congressional legislation applies only within the territorial borders of the United States unless specifically stated otherwise. Congress used clear language in the 1991 Act to expand coverage by amending the definition of "employee" in Title VII to mean a U.S. citizen employed in a foreign country by an American-owned or -controlled company. In short, an American now working overseas for a U.S.

company enjoys the same equal employment opportunity protection as an American working within the United States. Title VII, however, does not apply to foreign operations that are not owned or controlled by an American employer.

Limitation of Protection

The overseas extension of civil rights protections is not universal or automatic. A company is not required to comply with Title VII if compliance would cause the company to violate the law of the host country. For example, if a U.S. company has an operation in a foreign country that has statutes prohibiting the employment of women in management positions, Title VII would not apply. Because the company would be expected to follow the law of the host country, it could not be liable for sex discrimination under Title VII of the Civil Rights Act of 1964. This is in keeping with the well-established international law practice that countries may subject their own nationals to rules of conduct outside national borders as long as there is no conflict between those rules and the laws of the relevant foreign country. However, if the host country had no law explicitly stating such prohibition, the U.S. company is expected to ensure the U.S. mandated equal opportunities and protections of its U.S. employees.

Potential Effects

U.S. multinationals have been concerned about the effect that the extension of equal opportunity protections will have on their foreign operations. They are aware that there is an increased likelihood of litigation as female expatriates seek to protect their

overseas employment rights. Note that 70 percent of the respondents in a *Business Week* survey of 400 female managers thought women should take legal action if they see evidence of discrimination (Segal and Zellner 1992). The Civil Rights Act of 1991 has increased the geographic reach of both the protections and the remedies of women and ethnic and religious minorities.

A big problem for employers, and indirectly for female expatriates, arises when local custom creates gender barriers that are not overtly stated as national law. In such instances, Title VII would prevail and a female expatriate would be given access to the position even though such an assignment was contrary to host country social mores. The result could be the diminution of company/host country relations. This would be particularly likely if exporting U.S. equal employment philosophies is viewed as a form of "cultural imperialism" by the local community.

There could also be undesirable consequences for female expatriates themselves. For example, if a host country's culture makes sharp distinctions between what men are expected to do and what women are expected to do, U.S. female expatriates may encounter resistance if they are performing traditionally male roles. Failure to accept, or resentment of, the female expatriate's authority could hamper her ability to accomplish her assigned overseas mission. The question then becomes: How does a U.S. multinational obey U.S. law, meet its international staffing needs, and maintain good relations with its foreign host governments?

Plan of Action

In the spirit that preparation is better than litigation, we suggest a plan of action to aid employers. Guidelines that are well conceived, communicated clearly, and enforced throughout the organization offer the best prevention against lawsuits. The following action plan is designed to eliminate potential problems before they become cause for litigation.

- A corporation should sponsor reality training for managers who are or will be stationed abroad. Suitable subject matter should include the culture, values, and traditions of the host country and its people and how these facts may affect the manager. This information would be valuable for any potential expatriate, but particularly so to women and other groups who might be faced with special situations. For example, conduct that would be considered sexist here may not have the same connotation in the host culture. Corporate management, however, must be careful that the training is not used (or perceived to be used) to discourage women and minorities from international assignments. The sessions should include tactics to address potential difficulties, not merely an unbroken list of problems. An emphasis on realistic solutions or approaches is especially critical when the foreign environment is expected to be culturally hostile.

- There should be clear and consistent rules for use at the work site. Ongoing training for supervisors and managers already at the foreign location should be held regularly. The meaning and implementation effects of Title VII should be made familiar to all, including locals who hold supervisory positions. When possible, Title VII can be made explicit company policy at the site. Results of the training should be moni-

tored so that appropriate feedback can be given. Every effort should be made to make the foreign assignment a success for all concerned.

- Use local consultants to identify potential problems. No one will understand the traditions and habits of the local populace as well as one of the locals themselves. Consulting with a responsible consultant who is cognizant of the cultural artifacts and the needs of business will help an organization act rather than react to any difficulties.

- Consultants should clarify the legal status of local standard practices. If provisions regarding hiring and promoting are explicitly stated in the host country's laws, the company is not obligated under the Civil Rights Act to extend Title VII provisions to its employees in those matters. In fact, the company may be in jeopardy from the host country authorities if it imposes U.S. standards.

- If at all possible, avoid "token" situations. Fill multiple positions with women or minorities. A single appointment is often construed as a company's response to a perceived legal requirement, rather than as a commitment to promote the best regardless of gender or race. Additionally, filling multiple positions offers some protection against the necessity of maintaining a questionable employee from fear of lawsuit. The fact that others of the employee's gender or race are successfully remaining at the work site can offer some defense for the corporate action.

- Some foreign sites can be identified in advance as culturally hostile environments for certain groups of American citi-

zens. These societies impose severe restrictions—not necessarily written into law—on certain groups of people based on gender, religion, race, or national origin. A U.S. company can only protect its employees' rights within its jurisdiction. In a practical sense, that jurisdiction ends at the company "gate."

- Hiring locals for all management positions represents one method that would virtually eliminate the risk of assigning women and other minorities who may be doomed to failure by the severity of cultural circumstance. In the most culturally hostile environments, reliance on native-born managers may be the best answer. However, this must not be a half-hearted measure. The potential for charges of discrimination remains if the corporation fills lower-level positions with locals while the highest management positions are still reserved for the company's home office personnel. Remember that women constitute a growing number of such "home office personnel"; as such, they would therefore expect to be considered for the relevant positions.

Every day U.S. multinationals face increasing constraints in the development of their foreign operations. Many of their domestic-based managers are reluctant to accept international posts because of perceived disruptions in their personal and work lives.

At the same time, women managers are beginning to recognize the dearth of promotion opportunities within their companies and to see foreign posting as potentially beneficial. Their position for such advancement has been strengthened by the passage of the Civil Rights Act of 1991, which extends the Title VII rights of U.S. employees to work sites outside the boundaries of the country. These sites may be located in the midst of societies with strong cultural values that happen to conflict with U.S. standards.

Employers are, therefore, realistically concerned with their ability to balance the various constraints placed upon them. The guidelines we have proposed in this article should help provide these employees with a plan for action.

References

Nancy J. Adler, "Women in International Management: Where Are They?" *California Management Review*, 26, 4 (1984): 78–89.

Nancy J. Adler, "Women in Management Worldwide," *International Studies of Management and Organization*, 16, 3 (1986): 3–32.

J. Stewart Black, "Coming Home: The Relationship of Expatriate Expectations with Repatriation Adjustment and Job Performance," in Jerry L. Wall and Lawrence R. Jauch, eds., *Academy of Management Best Papers Proceedings 1991*: 91–95.

Joy Cherian, "Protecting Workers Overseas," *Journal of Commerce and Commercial*, November 25, 1991, p. A8.

Susan B. Garland, "Throwing Stones at the 'Glass Ceiling'," *Business Week*, August 19, 1991, p. 29.

Mariann Jelinek and Nancy J. Adler, "Women: World-Class Managers for Global Competition," *The Academy of Management Executive*, 11, 1 (1988): 11-9.

Lex K. Larson, *Civil Rights Act of 1991* (New York: Times-Mirror Books, 1992).

Kathryn E. Lewis and Pamela R. Johnson, "Preventing Sexual Harassment Complaints Based on Hostile Work Environments." *SAM Advanced Management Journal*, 56, 2 (1991): 21-26.

"Managers Balk at Overseas Assignments," *Wall Street Journal*, June 16, 1992, p. 1.

Amanda Troy Segal and Wendy Zellner, "Corporate Women," *Business Week*, June 8, 1992, pp. 74-83.

Raymond J. Stone, "Expatriate Selection and Failure," *Human Resource Planning*, 14, 1 (1991): 9-18.

Marilyn L. Taylor, Mariane Odjogov, and Eileen Morley, "Experienced American Professional Women in Overseas Business Assignments," *Academy of Management Proceedings*, 33 (1975): 454-456.

Rosalie Tung, "Career Issues in International Assignments," *The Academy of Management Executive*, 11, 3 (1988): 241-244.

Joseph Weber, "Farewell, Fast Track," *Business Week*, December 10, 1990, pp. 192-200.

QUESTIONS

1. What are some recent factors inhibiting managers from accepting foreign assignments?

2. Why have so few women been employed in foreign assignments?

3. When sending an expatriate to a country where a hostile environment exists for a certain class of employees, what might the company do to (a) comply with the new law and (b) help ensure success of the transferred expatriate?

4. What are the drawbacks of using only local managers in the foreign operations of companies?